Working Effectively with Unit Tests

Jay Fields

Working Effectively with Unit Tests

Jay Fields

This book is for sale at http://leanpub.com/wewut

This version was published on 2014-12-21

ISBN 978-1503242708

Leanpub

This is a Leanpub book. Leanpub empowers authors and publishers with the Lean Publishing process. Lean Publishing is the act of publishing an in-progress ebook using lightweight tools and many iterations to get reader feedback, pivot until you have the right book and build traction once you do.

Tweet This Book!

Please help Jay Fields by spreading the word about this book on Twitter!

The suggested hashtag for this book is #wewut.

Find out what other people are saying about the book by clicking on this link to search for this hashtag on Twitter:

https://twitter.com/search?q=#wewut

For Dana, the love of my life.

Contents

Foreword   i

Preface iii

Acknowledgments vii

Unit Testing, a First Example 1
    Thoughts on our Tests 9
    The Domain Code 12
    Moving Towards Readability 21
    Replace Loop with Individual Tests 24
    Expect Literals 31
    Inline Setup 36
    Replace ObjectMother with DataBuilder 40
    Comparing the Results 49
    Final Thoughts on our Tests 60

Motivators 63

Types of Tests 77
    State Verification 78
    Behavior Verification 81
    Unit Test 84
    Solitary Unit Test 85
    Sociable Unit Test 87

Continuing with Examples From Chapter 1 88
Final Thoughts, Again 108

Improving Assertions **131**
One Assertion Per Test 132
Implementation Overspecification 147
Assert Last 170
Expect Literals 181
Negative Testing 191
Hamcrest 198

Improving Test Cases **199**
Too Much Magic 201
Inline Setup 206
Test Names 227

Improving Test Suites **231**
Separating The Solitary From The Sociable 232
Questionable Tests 279
Custom Assertions 283
Global Definition 309

Closing Thoughts **329**
Broad Stack Tests 330
Test Pyramid 333
Final Thoughts On ROI 334
More... 336

Foreword

It's taken quite a while but we finally have consensus around the idea that unit testing is a necessity for most of today's projects. Occasionally, I see a voice in the wilderness challenge the idea - but just as quickly people who've been doing unit testing reflect back on their experience and notice the benefits that they've received. The idea of going without unit tests on a large project is just unthinkable for many people.

To me, this is success of the best kind - people are able to get more work done with less stress and fewer headaches. But that doesn't mean that it's all easy. Even though unit testing has been a strongly recommended practice since at least the early 2000s, people still struggle. They struggle because it is easy to get lost in the design decisions that you have to make when you are writing tests.

Tests are just as important as production code, but they are different. Through trial and error we are learning better practices but much of that knowledge is not yet widespread.

This is why I am very excited by Jay Fields' book. I've known Jay for close to a decade and over that time I've seen him approach problems in software with conscientiousness and deep curiosity - trying things out, discussing them and not being satisfied with answers that don't quite ring true. The book you're about to read is a culmination of that inquiry. Reading it, you'll learn a lot about unit testing. But, more than that, if you read between the lines you'll learn a lot about how to see and think about software.

– Michael Feathers, Director, R7K Research & Conveyance

Preface

Over a dozen years ago I read *Refactoring*[1] for the first time; it immediately became my bible. While *Refactoring* isn't about testing, it explicitly states: if you want to refactor, the essential precondition is having solid tests. At that time, if *Refactoring* deemed it necessary, I unquestionably complied. That was the beginning of my quest to create productive unit tests.

Throughout the 12+ years that followed my first reading of *Refactoring* I made many mistakes, learned countless lessons, and developed a set of guidelines that I believe make unit testing a productive use of programmer time. This book provides a single place to examine those mistakes, share the lessons learned, and provide direction in a way that I've found to be the most effective.

Why Test?

The answer was easy for me: *Refactoring* told me to. Unfortunately, doing something strictly because someone or something told you to is possibly the worst approach you could take. The more time I've invested in testing, the more I've found myself returning to the question: Why am I writing this test?

---

[1]http://martinfowler.com/books/refactoring.html

There are many motivators for creating a test or several tests:

- validate the system
  - immediate feedback that things work as expected
  - prevent future regressions
- increase code-coverage
- enable refactoring
- document the behavior of the system
- your manager told you to
- Test Driven Development
  - improved design
  - breaking a problem up into smaller pieces
  - defining the "simplest thing that could possibly work"
- customer acceptance
- ping pong pair-programming

Some of the above motivators are healthy in the right context, others are indicators of larger problems. Before writing any test, I would recommend deciding which of the above are motivating your testing. If you first understand why you're writing a test, you'll have a much better chance of writing a test that is maintainable and will make you more productive in the long run.

Once you start looking at tests while considering the motivator, you may find you have tests that aren't actually making you more productive. For example, you may have a test that increases code-coverage, but satisfies no other motivator. If your team requires 100% code-coverage, then the test provides value. However, if your team has abandoned the (in my opinion harmful) goal of 100% code-coverage, then you're in a position to perform my favorite refactoring: delete.

Who Should Read This Book

This book is aimed at a professional programmer, someone who writes software for a living. The examples and discussion include a lot of code to read and to understand.

Although this book is focused on testing, testable code can have a large impact on the design of a system. It is vital for senior designers and architects to understand the principles recommended and to use them in their projects. The principles within this book are best introduced to a team by a respected and experienced developer. Such a developer can best understand the principles and adapt them to their specific context. In addition, familiarity with this book's content will allow experienced developers to provide it as a reference for the less experienced members of their team.

Despite my opinion on who should introduce these concepts, I've attempted to write this book for both people experienced with and those brand-new to unit testing. Ideally, a respected programmer will look to implement the ideas within this book, and begin by passing this book on to those on the team that would likely share interest in this approach. If you're already writing tests I believe this book will provide concepts and suggestions that will prove useful for years to come. If you aren't already writing tests you'll likely want to pick up an intro to unit testing book as well. The concepts in this book should be understandable to developers of all levels; however, we will not cover concepts such as framework selection, framework configuration, or writing your first test.

Building on the Foundations Laid by Others

While this book does contain an Acknowledgments section, it wouldn't be practical to thank everyone that has contributed to creating the practices that this book details. I can say with full confidence that I wouldn't be in the position to write this book without at least the following groups:

- creators and maintainers of both NUnit and JUnit
- creators and maintainers of NMock, (James Mead's) Mocha, Mockito, JMock, and RSpec
- each team member from each of my projects at Thought-Works & DRW Trading
- every conference speaker or attendee who's provided feedback on my (sometimes radical) ideas
- every person who left a comment on blog.jayfields.com[2]

Thank you all, I deeply appreciate the feedback you've given throughout the years.

---

[2]http://blog.jayfields.com

Acknowledgments

After writing *Refactoring: Ruby Edition*, I swore I'd never write another book. Book writing is unquestionably a labor of love, and I wouldn't be able to do it without the support of my many friends in the industry.

- Martin Fowler: Thank you for allowing me to reference and reuse content from *Refactoring*. It's still my favorite technical book of all time.
- Obie Fernandez: Thank you for the nudge to use leanpub; it was crucial for making this project happen.
- Michael Feathers: Honestly, I just liked the way *Working Effectively with Unit Tests* sounded. I never considered that anyone would associate this book with a book as universally loved as *Working Effectively with Legacy Code*. Nonetheless, I'll do my best to deliver a book that is worthy of being on the same shelf as *Working Effectively with Legacy Code*. Thank you very much for your blessing.
- Original Reviewers: There's no question this book is significantly better due to the feedback I got from those who originally volunteered to provide feedback. Thank you Graham Nash, John Hume, Pat Farley, & Steve McLarnon.

Additionally, I've been happily surprised by the support I've gotten from people who purchased the early edition on leanpub and promptly provided feedback. Many thanks - Allan Clarke, Corey Haines, Derek Reeve, J. B. Rainsberger, Jake McCrary, Josh Graham, Kent Spillner, & Steve Vinoski.

I'm sure there are others who I've forgotten; I apologize and offer my thanks.

Unit Testing, a First Example

I'd like to begin this book with an example, and I believe Martin's description of why is as clear as it can be written:

> Traditionally technical books start with a general introduction that outlines things like history and broad principles. When someone does that at a conference, I get slightly sleepy. My mind starts wandering with a low-priority background process that polls the speaker until he or she gives an example. The examples wake me up because it is with examples that I can see what is going on. With principles it is too easy to make generalizations, too hard to figure out how to apply things. An example helps make things clear. –Martin Fowler, Refactoring: Ruby Edition

Note: If the following domain looks familiar to you, that's because I've borrowed it from *Refactoring*.

Without further ado, I present a test failure.

```
JUnit version 4.11
.E.E..
There were 2 failures:
1) statement(CustomerTest)
org.junit.ComparisonFailure: expected:<...or John
        Godfather 4[          ]9.0
Amount owed is 9...> but was:<...or John
        Godfather 4[ ]9.0
Amount owed is 9...>
2) htmlStatement(CustomerTest)
org.junit.ComparisonFailure: expected:<...</h1>
<p>Godfather 4[          ]9.0</p>
<p>Amount ow...> but was:<...</h1>
<p>Godfather 4[ ]9.0</p>
<p>Amount ow...>

FAILURES!!!
Tests run: 4,   Failures: 2
```

The above output is what JUnit will report (sans stacktrace noise) for the (soon to follow) CustomerTest class.

Unless you work alone and on greenfield projects exclusively, you'll often find your first introduction to a test will be when it fails. If that's a common case you'll encounter at work then it feels like a great way to start the book as well.

Below you'll find the cause of the failure, the CustomerTest class.

```java
public class CustomerTest {
  Customer john, steve, pat, david;
  String johnName = "John",
    steveName = "Steve",
    patName = "Pat",
    davidName = "David";
  Customer[] customers;

  @Before
  public void setup() {
    david = ObjectMother
      .customerWithNoRentals(
        davidName);
    john = ObjectMother
      .customerWithOneNewRelease(
        johnName);
    pat = ObjectMother
      .customerWithOneOfEachRentalType(
        patName);
    steve = ObjectMother
      .customerWithOneNewReleaseAndOneRegular(
        steveName);
    customers =
      new Customer[]
      { david, john, steve, pat};
  }
```

```
@Test
public void getName() {
  assertEquals(
    davidName, david.getName());
  assertEquals(
    johnName, john.getName());
  assertEquals(
    steveName, steve.getName());
  assertEquals(
    patName, pat.getName());
}

@Test
public void statement() {
  for (int i=0; i<customers.length; i++) {
    assertEquals(
      expStatement(
        "Rental record for %s\n" +
        "%sAmount owed is %s\n"  +
        "You earned %s frequent " +
        "renter points",
        customers[i],
        rentalInfo(
          "\t", "",
          customers[i].getRentals())),
      customers[i].statement());
  }
}
```

```java
@Test
public void htmlStatement() {
  for (int i=0; i<customers.length; i++) {
    assertEquals(
      expStatement(
        "<h1>Rental record for " +
        "<em>%s</em></h1>\n%s" +
        "<p>Amount owed is <em>%s</em>" +
        "</p>\n<p>You earned <em>%s" +
        " frequent renter points</em></p>",
        customers[i],
        rentalInfo(
          "<p>", "</p>",
          customers[i].getRentals())),
      customers[i].htmlStatement());
  }
}

@Test
(expected=IllegalArgumentException.class)
public void invalidTitle() {
  ObjectMother
    .customerWithNoRentals("Bob")
    .addRental(
      new Rental(
        new Movie("Crazy, Stupid, Love.",
                  Movie.Type.UNKNOWN),
        4));
}
```

```java
public static String rentalInfo(
  String startsWith,
  String endsWith,
  List<Rental> rentals) {
  String result = "";
  for (Rental rental : rentals)
    result += String.format(
      "%s%s\t%s%s\n",
      startsWith,
      rental.getMovie().getTitle(),
      rental.getCharge(),
      endsWith);
  return result;
}

public static String expStatement(
  String formatStr,
  Customer customer,
  String rentalInfo) {
  return String.format(
    formatStr,
    customer.getName(),
    rentalInfo,
    customer.getTotalCharge(),
    customer.getTotalPoints());
  }
}
```

The CustomerTest class completely covers our Customer domain object and has very little duplication; many would consider this a well written set of tests.

As you can see, we're using an ObjectMother to create our domain objects. The following code represents the full definition of our ObjectMother class.

```java
public class ObjectMother {
  public static Customer
  customerWithOneOfEachRentalType(
    String name) {
    Customer result =
      customerWithOneNewReleaseAndOneRegular(
        name);
    result.addRental(
      new Rental(
        new Movie("Lion King", CHILDREN), 3));
    return result;
  }

  public static Customer
  customerWithOneNewReleaseAndOneRegular(
    String n) {
    Customer result =
      customerWithOneNewRelease(n);
    result.addRental(
      new Rental(
        new Movie("Scarface", REGULAR), 3));
    return result;
  }
```

```java
public static Customer
customerWithOneNewRelease(
  String name) {
  Customer result =
    customerWithNoRentals(name);
  result.addRental(
    new Rental(
      new Movie(
        "Godfather 4", NEW_RELEASE), 3));
  return result;
}

public static Customer
customerWithNoRentals(String name) {
  return new Customer(name);
}
}
```

Thoughts on our Tests

Our CustomerTest class is written in a way that follows many common patterns. It doesn't take much searching on the Web to find articles giving examples of "improving" your code by using a Setup (now @Before in JUnit). ObjectMother lives under many names, and each name comes with several articles explaining how it's either successful or the programmer didn't understand how to correctly apply the pattern. Our tests follow the common advice that above all, code must be DRY[3].

> DRY is an acronym for Don't Repeat Yourself, and is defined as: *Every piece of knowledge must have a single, unambiguous, authoritative representation within a system.*

Both of those pieces of advice are contextually valuable. I can easily think of situations where applying each of those patterns would be the right choice. However, in the context of "I would like to quickly understand this test I've never seen before", those patterns come up short. While working on code written by a teammate or supporting an inherited system, I find myself in the latter context far more often than not.

I suspect most people will have skimmed the above tests - that's what I would have done. Other people may have taken the time to try to understand the test and how it relates to the failure output. If you're in the second group, I suspect your thought process might have looked something like this.

---

[3]http://en.wikipedia.org/wiki/Don't_repeat_yourself

1. find the `statement` test
2. find the definition of the `customers` array that we're iterating
3. find the assignment to `customers`
4. digest the assignment of each `Customer` and their associated name
5. look to `ObjectMother` to determine how the `Customer` instances are created
6. digest each of the different `Customer` instance creation methods within the `ObjectMother`
   - you now understand the first line of the test
7. digest that the expected value is being created by calling a method with a `String`, a `Customer`, and the result of calling `rentalInfo` with 2 `String` instances and a customer's `rentals`.
8. find the `rentalInfo` method and determine what value it's returning to `expStatement`
9. digest that `rentalInfo` is creating a string by iterating and formatting `Rental` data
10. now that you've mentally resolved the args to `expStatement`, you find that method and digest it.
    - at this point it's taken 10 steps to simply understand the expected value in your test
11. recognize that the actual value is a call to the domain object, who's source I haven't supplied (yet).

That's quite a bit you needed to digest, and all of it test code. Not one character of what you've digested will actually run in production.

Were you actually trying to fix this test, the next logical question would be: which is incorrect, the expected value or the actual value? Unfortunately, before you could even begin to tackle that question you'd need to find out what the expected and actual values actually are. We can see the text differs around the word "Godfather", but that only narrows our list down to the customers john, steve, and pat. It's practically impossible to fix this test without writing some code and/or using the debugger for runtime inspection to help you identify the issue.

The Domain Code

Below you will find the domain code from Refactoring rewritten for Java 7. It's not necessary to digest the domain code now to complete this chapter. I would recommend skimming or completely skipping to the end of the section, and coming back to use this as a reference only if you want to verify your understanding of the code under test.

```
public class Customer {

  private String name;
  private List<Rental> rentals =
    new ArrayList<Rental>();

  public Customer(String name) {
    this.name = name;
  }

  public String getName() {
    return name;
  }

  public List<Rental> getRentals() {
    return rentals;
  }

  public void addRental(Rental rental) {
    rentals.add(rental);
  }
```

```
public String statement() {
  String result =
    "Rental record for " + getName() + "\n";
  for (Rental rental : rentals)
    result +=
      "\t" + rental.getLineItem() + "\n";
  result +=
    "Amount owed is " + getTotalCharge() +
    "\n" + "You earned " +
    getTotalPoints() +
    " frequent renter points";
  return result;
}

public String htmlStatement() {
  String result =
    "<h1>Rental record for <em>" +
    getName() + "</em></h1>\n";
  for (Rental rental : rentals)
    result += "<p>" + rental.getLineItem() +
      "</p>\n";
  result +=
    "<p>Amount owed is <em>" +
    getTotalCharge() + "</em></p>\n" +
    "<p>You earned <em>" +
    getTotalPoints() +
    " frequent renter points</em></p>";
  return result;

}
```

```
public double getTotalCharge() {
  double total = 0;
  for (Rental rental : rentals)
    total += rental.getCharge();
  return total;
}

public int getTotalPoints() {
  int total = 0;
  for (Rental rental : rentals)
    total += rental.getPoints();
  return total;
}
}
```

```java
public class Rental {

  Movie movie;
  private int daysRented;

  public Rental(Movie movie, int daysRented) {
    this.movie = movie;
    this.daysRented = daysRented;
  }

  public Movie getMovie() {
    return movie;
  }

  public int getDaysRented() {
    return daysRented;
  }

  public double getCharge() {
    return movie.getCharge(daysRented);
  }

  public int getPoints() {
    return movie.getPoints(daysRented);
  }

  public String getLineItem() {
    return
      movie.getTitle() + " " + getCharge();
  }
}
```

```java
public class Movie {

  public enum Type {
    REGULAR, NEW_RELEASE, CHILDREN, UNKNOWN;
  }

  private String title;
  Price price;

  public Movie(
    String title, Movie.Type priceCode) {
    this.title = title;
    setPriceCode(priceCode);
  }

  public String getTitle() {
    return title;
  }
```

```java
  private void setPriceCode(
    Movie.Type priceCode) {
    switch (priceCode) {
    case CHILDREN:
      price = new ChildrensPrice();
      break;
    case NEW_RELEASE:
      price = new NewReleasePrice();
      break;
    case REGULAR:
      price = new RegularPrice();
      break;
    default:
      throw new IllegalArgumentException(
        "invalid price code");
    }
  }

  public double getCharge(int daysRented) {
    return price.getCharge(daysRented);
  }

  public int getPoints(int daysRented) {
    return price.getPoints(daysRented);
  }
}
```

```java
public abstract class Price {
  abstract double getCharge(int daysRented);

  int getPoints(int daysRented) {
    return 1;
  }
}


public class ChildrensPrice extends Price {
  @Override
  double getCharge(int daysRented) {
    double amount = 1.5;
    if (daysRented > 3)
      amount += (daysRented - 3) * 1.5;
    return amount;
  }
}
```

```java
public class RegularPrice extends Price {
  @Override
  public double getCharge(int daysRented) {
    double amount = 2;
    if (daysRented > 2)
      amount += (daysRented - 2) * 1.5;
    return amount;
  }
}


public class NewReleasePrice extends Price {
  @Override
  public double getCharge(int daysRented) {
    return daysRented * 3;
  }

  @Override
  int getPoints(int daysRented) {
    if (daysRented > 1)
      return 2;
    return 1;
  }
}
```

Moving Towards Readability

When asked "Why do you test?", industry veteran Josh Graham gave the following answer:

> To create a tiny universe where the software exists to do one thing and do it well.

The example tests could have been written for many reasons, let's assume the motivators that matter to us are: enable refactoring, immediate feedback, and breaking a problem up into smaller pieces. The tests fit well for our first two motivators, but fail to do a good job of breaking a problem up into smaller pieces. When writing these tests it's obvious and clear where "duplication" lies and how "common" pieces can be pulled into helper methods. Unfortunately, each time we extract a method we risk complicating our tiny universes. The right abstractions can reduce complexity; however, it's often unclear which abstraction within a test will provide the most value to the team.

DRY has been applied to the tests as it would be to production code. At first glance this may seem like a reasonable approach; however, test code and production code is written, maintained, and reviewed in drastically different ways. Production code collaborates to provide a single running application, and it's generally wise to avoid duplicating concepts within that application. Tests do not, or at least should not collaborate; it's universally accepted that inter-test dependency is an anti-pattern. If we think of tests as tiny, independent universes, then code that appears in one test should not necessarily be considered inadvisable duplication if it appears in another test as well.

Still, I recognize that pragmatic removal of duplication can add to maintainability. The examples that follow will address issues such as *We've grouped david, john, pat, & steve despite the fact that none of them interact with each other in any way whatsoever* not by duplicating every character, but by introducing local and global patterns that I find superior.

When I think about the current state of the tests, I remember my colleague Pat Farley describing some tests as having been *made DRY with a blowtorch.*

Rather than viewing our tests as a single interconnected program, we can shift our focus to viewing each test as a tiny universe; each test can be an individual procedural program that has a single responsibility. If we want to keep our individual procedural programs as tiny universes, we'll likely make many decisions differently.

- We won't test diverse customers at the same time.
- We won't create diverse customers that have nothing to do with each other.
- We won't extract methods for a single string return value.
- We'll create data where we need it, not as part of a special framework method.

In general, I find applying DRY to a subset of tests to be an anti-pattern. Within a single test, DRY can often apply. Likewise, globally appropriate DRY application is often a good choice. However, once you start applying DRY at a test group level you often increase the complexity of your individual procedures where a local or global solution would have been superior.

For those that enjoy acronyms, when writing tests you should prefer DAMP (Descriptive And Maintainable Procedures) to DRY.

The remainder of the chapter will demonstrate the individual steps we can take to create tests so small they become trivial to immediately understand.

Replace Loop with Individual Tests

The first step in moving to more readable tests is breaking the iteration into individual tests. The following code provides the same regression protection and immediate feedback as the original, while also explicitly giving us more information: passing and failing assertions that may give additional clues as to where the problem exists.

```java
public class CustomerTest {
  Customer john, steve, pat, david;
  String johnName = "John",
    steveName = "Steve",
    patName = "Pat",
    davidName = "David";
  Customer[] customers;

  @Before
  public void setup() {
    david = ObjectMother
      .customerWithNoRentals(davidName);
    john = ObjectMother
      .customerWithOneNewRelease(johnName);
    pat = ObjectMother
      .customerWithOneOfEachRentalType(
        patName);
    steve = ObjectMother
      .customerWithOneNewReleaseAndOneRegular(
        steveName);
    customers = new Customer[] {
      david, john, steve, pat };
  }
```

```java
@Test
public void davidStatement() {
  assertEquals(
    expStatement(
      "Rental record for %s\n%sAmount " +
      "owed is %s\nYou earned %s " +
      "frequent renter points",
      david,
      rentalInfo(
        "\t", "", david.getRentals())),
    david.statement());
}


@Test
public void johnStatement() {
  assertEquals(
    expStatement(
      "Rental record for %s\n%sAmount " +
      "owed is %s\nYou earned %s " +
      "frequent renter points",
      john,
      rentalInfo(
        "\t", "", john.getRentals())),
    john.statement());
}
```

```
@Test
public void patStatement() {
  assertEquals(
    expStatement(
      "Rental record for %s\n%sAmount " +
      "owed is %s\nYou earned %s " +
      "frequent renter points",
      pat,
      rentalInfo(
        "\t", "", pat.getRentals())),
    pat.statement());
}

@Test
public void steveStatement() {
  assertEquals(
    expStatement(
      "Rental record for %s\n%s" +
      "Amount owed is %s\nYou earned %s " +
      "frequent renter points",
      steve,
      rentalInfo(
        "\t", "", steve.getRentals())),
    steve.statement());
}
```

```java
public static String rentalInfo(
  String startsWith,
  String endsWith,
  List<Rental> rentals) {
  String result = "";
  for (Rental rental : rentals)
    result += String.format(
      "%s%s\t%s%s\n",
      startsWith,
      rental.getMovie().getTitle(),
      rental.getCharge(),
      endsWith);
  return result;
}

public static String expStatement(
  String formatStr,
  Customer customer,
  String rentalInfo) {
  return String.format(
    formatStr,
    customer.getName(),
    rentalInfo,
    customer.getTotalCharge(),
    customer.getTotalPoints());
  }
}
```

The following output is the result of running the above test.

```
JUnit version 4.11
.E.E..E
There were 3 failures:
1) johnStatement(CustomerTest)
org.junit.ComparisonFailure: expected:<...or John
        Godfather 4[          ]9.0
Amount owed is 9...> but was:<...or John
        Godfather 4[ ]9.0
Amount owed is 9...>
2) steveStatement(CustomerTest)
org.junit.ComparisonFailure: expected:<...r Steve
        Godfather 4[          9.0
        Scarface          ]3.5
Amount owed is 1...> but was:<...r Steve
        Godfather 4[ 9.0
        Scarface ]3.5
Amount owed is 1...>
3) patStatement(CustomerTest)
org.junit.ComparisonFailure: expected:<...for Pat
        Godfather 4[          9.0
        Scarface          3.5
        Lion King          ]1.5
Amount owed is 1...> but was:<...for Pat
        Godfather 4[ 9.0
        Scarface 3.5
        Lion King ]1.5
Amount owed is 1...>

FAILURES!!!
Tests run: 4, Failures: 3
```

At this point we have more clues about which tests are failing and where; specifically, we know that davidStatement is

passing, so the issue must exist in the printing of rental information. Unfortunately, we don't currently have any strings to
quickly look at to determine whether the error exists in our
expected or actual values.

Expect Literals

The next step in increasing readability is expecting literal values. If you know where the problem exists, having DRY tests can help ensure you type the fewest number of characters. That said...

> "Programming is not about typing... it's about thinking." –Rich Hickey

At this point, our tests have become much smaller universes, so small that I find myself wondering why I call a parameterized method, once, that does nothing more than return a `String`. Within my tiny universe it would be much easier to simply use a `String` literal.

A few printlns and copy-pastes later, my tests are much more explicit, and my universes have gotten even smaller.

```java
public class CustomerTest {
  Customer john, steve, pat, david;
  String johnName = "John",
    steveName = "Steve",
    patName = "Pat",
    davidName = "David";
  Customer[] customers;

  @Before
  public void setup() {
    david = ObjectMother
      .customerWithNoRentals(davidName);
    john = ObjectMother
      .customerWithOneNewRelease(johnName);
    pat = ObjectMother
      .customerWithOneOfEachRentalType(
        patName);
    steve = ObjectMother
      .customerWithOneNewReleaseAndOneRegular(
        steveName);
    customers = new Customer[] {
      david, john, steve, pat };
  }

  @Test
  public void davidStatement() {
    assertEquals(
      "Rental record for David\nAmount " +
      "owed is 0.0\n" +
      "You earned 0 frequent renter points",
      david.statement());
  }
```

```
@Test
public void johnStatement() {
  assertEquals(
    "Rental record for John\n\t" +
    "Godfather 4\t9.0\n" +
    "Amount owed is 9.0\n" +
    "You earned 2 frequent renter points",
    john.statement());
}

@Test
public void patStatement() {
  assertEquals(
    "Rental record for Pat\n\t" +
    "Godfather 4\t9.0\n" +
    "\tScarface\t3.5\n" +
    "\tLion King\t1.5\n" +
    "Amount owed is 14.0\n" +
    "You earned 4 frequent renter points",
    pat.statement());
}
```

```
@Test
public void steveStatement() {
  assertEquals(
    "Rental record for Steve\n\t" +
    "Godfather 4\t9.0\n" +
    "\tScarface\t3.5\n" +
    "Amount owed is 12.5\n" +
    "You earned 3 frequent renter points",
    steve.statement());
  }
}
```

The failure output is exactly the same, but I'm now able to look at the expected value as a simple constant, and reduce my first question to: is my expected value correct? For those coding along: we'll assume the *"fix"* for the failure is to change the expected value to match the implementation in Rental.getLineItem (space delimited). The expected values moving forward will reflect this *fix*.

> note: Some reviewers were offended by the getRentals public method (though others were not). If a method such as getRentals is something you'd look to remove from your domain model, then the *Expect Literals* refactoring provides you with at least two benefits: the one you've already seen, and the ability to delete the getRentals method entirely. These types of improvements (deleting code while also improving expressiveness is always an improvement, regardless of your preferred OO style) are not uncommon; improving tests often allows you to improve your domain model as well.

There's an entire section dedicated to Expect Literals in Improving Assertions

If this were more than a book example, my next step would likely be adding fine grained tests that verify individual methods of each of the classes that are collaborating with Customer. Unfortunately, moving in that direction will first require discussion on the benefits of fine grained tests and the trade-offs of using mocks and stubs.

If you're interested in jumping straight to this discussion it can be found in the Types of Tests chapter.

Inline Setup

At this point it should be easy to find the source of the failing test; however, our universes aren't quite DAMP just yet.

Have you ever stopped to ask yourself why we use a design pattern (Template Method) in our tests, when an explicit method call is probably the appropriate choice 99% of the time?

Creating instances of david, john, pat, & steve in Setup moves characters out of the individual test methods, but doesn't provide us any other advantage. It also comes with the conceptual overhead of each Customer being created, whether or not it's used. By adding a level of indirection we've removed characters from tests, but we've forced ourselves to remember who has what rentals. Removing a setup method almost always reveals an opportunity for a local or global improvement within a universe.

In this case, by removing Setup we're able to further limit the number of variables that require inspection when you first encounter a test. With Setup removed you no longer need to look for a Setup method, and you no longer need to care about the Customer instances that are irrelevant to your tiny universe.

```java
public class CustomerTest {
  @Test
  public void noRentalsStatement() {
    assertEquals(
      "Rental record for David\nAmount " +
      "owed is 0.0\n" +
      "You earned 0 frequent renter points",
      ObjectMother
      .customerWithNoRentals(
        "David").statement());
  }

  @Test
  public void oneNewReleaseStatement() {
    assertEquals(
      "Rental record for John\n\t" +
      "Godfather 4 9.0\n" +
      "Amount owed is 9.0\n" +
      "You earned 2 frequent renter points",
      ObjectMother
      .customerWithOneNewRelease(
        "John").statement());
  }
```

```
@Test
public void allRentalTypesStatement() {
  assertEquals(
    "Rental record for Pat\n\t" +
    "Godfather 4 9.0\n" +
    "\tScarface 3.5\n\tLion King 1.5\n" +
    "Amount owed is 14.0\n" +
    "You earned 4 frequent renter points",
    ObjectMother
    .customerWithOneOfEachRentalType(
      "Pat").statement());
}


@Test
public void
newReleaseAndRegularStatement() {
  assertEquals(
    "Rental record for Steve\n\t" +
    "Godfather 4 9.0\n" +
    "\tScarface 3.5\n" +
    "Amount owed is 12.5\n" +
    "You earned 3 frequent renter points",
    ObjectMother
    .customerWithOneNewReleaseAndOneRegular(
      "Steve").statement());
}
}
```

By Inlining Setup we get to delete both the Setup method and the Customer fields. Our tests are looking nice and slim, and they require almost no navigation to completely understand. I went ahead and renamed the tests, deleted the unused customers field, and inlined the single usage fields.

It's confession time: I don't like test names. Technically they're method names, but they're **never** called explicitly. That alone should make you somewhat suspicious. I consider method names found within tests to be glorified comments that come with all the standard warnings: they often grow out of date, and are often a Code Smell[4] emanating from bad code. Unfortunately, most testing frameworks make test names mandatory, and you *should* spend the time to create helpful test names. While we refactored away from the looping test I lazily named my tests based on the customer; however, I was forced to create a more appropriate name as a side effect of performing Inline Setup.

I believe this is another example of how well written tests have side effects that improve associated code. I've personally written testing frameworks that make test names optional, that's how little I care about test names. Still, once I performed Inline Setup, the only reasonable choice was to create a somewhat helpful test name.

Our tests are looking better and better, and I'm feeling motivated to continue the evolution. There's still one additional step I would take.

---

[4]http://en.wikipedia.org/wiki/Code_smell

Replace ObjectMother with DataBuilder

ObjectMother is an effective tool when the scenarios are limited and constant, but there's no clear way to handle the situation when you need a slightly different scenario. For example, if you wanted to create a test for the statement method on a Customer with two New Releases, would you add another ObjectMother method or would you call the addRental method on an instance returned?

Further complicating the issue: it's often hard to know if you're dealing with objects that you can manipulate or if the objects returned from an ObjectMother are reused. For example, if you called ObjectMother.customerWithTwoNewReleases, can you change the name on one of the New Release instances, or was the same Movie supplied to addRental twice? You can't know without looking at the implementation.

At this point it would be natural to delete the ObjectMother and simply create your domain model instances using new. If the number of calls to new within your tests will be limited, that's the pragmatic path. However, as the number of calls to new grows so does the risk of needing to do a cascading update. Say you have less than a dozen calls to new Customer(...) in your tests and you need to add a constructor argument, updating those dozen or less calls will not severely impact your effectiveness. Conversely, if you have one hundred calls to new Customer(...) and you add a constructor argument, you're now forced to update the code in one hundred different places.

A DataBuilder is an alternative to a scenario based ObjectMother that also addresses the cascading update risk. The following a class is a DataBuilder that will allow us to build our domain objects that aren't tied to any particular scenario.

(I recommend skimming the following builder, we'll revisit *Test Data Builders* in detail in the TestDataBuilder section of Chapter 6)

```
public class a {
  public static CustomerBuilder customer =
    new CustomerBuilder();
  public static RentalBuilder rental =
    new RentalBuilder();
  public static MovieBuilder movie =
    new MovieBuilder();

  public static class CustomerBuilder {
    Rental[] rentals;
    String name;

    CustomerBuilder() {
      this("Jim", new Rental[0]);
    }

    CustomerBuilder(
      String name, Rental[] rentals) {
      this.name = name;
      this.rentals = rentals;
    }

    public CustomerBuilder w(
      RentalBuilder... builders) {
      Rental[] rentals =
        new Rental[builders.length];
```

```
    for (int i=0; i<builders.length; i++) {
      rentals[i] = builders[i].build();
    }
    return
      new CustomerBuilder(name, rentals);
  }

  public CustomerBuilder w(String name) {
    return
      new CustomerBuilder(name, rentals);
  }

  public Customer build() {
    Customer result = new Customer(name);
    for (Rental rental : rentals) {
      result.addRental(rental);
    }
    return result;
  }
}
```

```java
public static class RentalBuilder {
  final Movie movie;
  final int days;

  RentalBuilder() {
    this(new MovieBuilder().build(), 3);
  }

  RentalBuilder(Movie movie, int days) {
    this.movie = movie;
    this.days = days;
  }

  public RentalBuilder w(
    MovieBuilder movie) {
    return
      new RentalBuilder(
        movie.build(), days);
  }

  public Rental build() {
    return new Rental(movie, days);
  }
}
```

```java
public static class MovieBuilder {
  final String name;
  final Movie.Type type;

  MovieBuilder() {
    this("Godfather 4",
         Movie.Type.NEW_RELEASE);
  }

  MovieBuilder(
    String name, Movie.Type type) {
    this.name = name;
    this.type = type;
  }

  public MovieBuilder w(Movie.Type type) {
    return new MovieBuilder(name, type);
  }

  public MovieBuilder w(String name) {
    return new MovieBuilder(name, type);
  }

  public Movie build() {
    return new Movie(name, type);
  }
}
}
```

The a class is undeniably longer than an ObjectMother; however it's not only more general it also puts the decision in your hands to share or not share an object. Let's look at what our test could look like when utilizing a *Test Data Builder.*

note: w( ) is an abbreviation for with( ).

```java
public class CustomerTest {
  @Test
  public void noRentalsStatement() {
    assertEquals(
      "Rental record for David\nAmount " +
      "owed is 0.0\nYou earned 0 frequent " +
      "renter points",
      a.customer.w(
        "David").build().statement());
  }

  @Test
  public void oneNewReleaseStatement() {
    assertEquals(
      "Rental record for John\n\t" +
      "Godfather 4 9.0\nAmount owed is " +
      "9.0\nYou earned 2 frequent renter " +
      "points",
      a.customer.w("John").w(
        a.rental.w(
          a.movie.w(NEW_RELEASE))).build()
      .statement());
  }
```

```java
@Test
public void allRentalTypesStatement() {
  assertEquals(
    "Rental record for Pat\n\t" +
    "Godfather 4 9.0\n\tScarface 3.5\n" +
    "\tLion King 1.5\nAmount owed is " +
    "14.0\nYou earned 4 frequent renter " +
    "points",
    a.customer.w("Pat").w(
      a.rental.w(a.movie.w(NEW_RELEASE)),
      a.rental.w(a.movie.w("Scarface").w(
                 REGULAR)),
      a.rental.w(a.movie.w("Lion King").w(
                 CHILDREN))).build()
    .statement());
}
```

```
@Test
public void
newReleaseAndRegularStatement() {
  assertEquals(
    "Rental record for Steve\n\t" +
    "Godfather 4 9.0\n\tScarface 3.5\n" +
    "Amount owed is 12.5\nYou earned 3 " +
    "frequent renter points",
    a.customer.w("Steve").w(
      a.rental.w(a.movie.w(NEW_RELEASE)),
      a.rental.w(
        a.movie.w(
          "Scarface").w(REGULAR))).build()
    .statement());
  }
}
```

The above test is functionally equivalent to all the previous test methods used to verify statement. This version does require us to understand the abstract concept and concrete implementation of a *Test Data Builder*; however, there's no guarantee that you would need to visit the a class to understand this test - even the first time you encounter the test. The a class is a class used globally to create all domain objects for all tests. With that kind of scope, unless this is your first day on a project, it's not really possible that you wouldn't have encountered the a class in the past.

To be more clear, the lone responsibility of a *Test Data Builder* is to create domain objects with default values. Thus, even if you've never seen this test before, without navigating to a you'll already know that you're creating a customer with sensible defaults. This is a rare example of an abstraction that, despite adding indirection, also makes the test easier to digest.

With a *Test Data Builder* in place it becomes trivial to add an additional test that verifies the case of 2 New Releases, or any other rental combination that you find to be important.

As I previously mentioned, the choice to use a *Test Data Builder* will likely depend on the number of calls to new and your tolerance for cascading update risk. I introduce them here due to their frequent usage throughout the book. In practice I like to use new while there are half a dozen or fewer calls to a constructor.

More information on *Test Data Builders* can be found in Nat Pryce's article on Test Data Builders[5] and by skipping directly to the TestDataBuilder section of Chapter 6.

---

[5]http://www.natpryce.com/articles/000714.html

Comparing the Results

> Any fool can write code that a computer can understand. Good programmers write code that humans can understand. –Martin Fowler, Refactoring.

> Applied to Unit Testing: Any fool can write a test that helps them today. Good programmers write tests that help the entire team in the future.

Below you can find both the before and after examples, allowing a quick comparison.

Original

```java
public class CustomerTest {
  Customer john, steve, pat, david;
  String johnName = "John",
    steveName = "Steve",
    patName = "Pat",
    davidName = "David";
  Customer[] customers;

  @Before
  public void setup() {
    david = ObjectMother
      .customerWithNoRentals(
        davidName);
    john = ObjectMother
      .customerWithOneNewRelease(
        johnName);
    pat = ObjectMother
      .customerWithOneOfEachRentalType(
        patName);
    steve = ObjectMother
      .customerWithOneNewReleaseAndOneRegular(
        steveName);
    customers =
      new Customer[]
      { david, john, steve, pat};
  }
```

```java
@Test
public void getName() {
  assertEquals(
    davidName, david.getName());
  assertEquals(
    johnName, john.getName());
  assertEquals(
    steveName, steve.getName());
  assertEquals(
    patName, pat.getName());
}

@Test
public void statement() {
  for (int i=0; i<customers.length; i++) {
    assertEquals(
      expStatement(
        "Rental record for %s\n" +
        "%sAmount owed is %s\n"  +
        "You earned %s frequent " +
        "renter points",
        customers[i],
        rentalInfo(
          "\t", "",
          customers[i].getRentals())),
      customers[i].statement());
  }
}
```

```java
@Test
public void htmlStatement() {
  for (int i=0; i<customers.length; i++) {
    assertEquals(
      expStatement(
        "<h1>Rental record for " +
        "<em>%s</em></h1>\n%s" +
        "<p>Amount owed is <em>%s</em>" +
        "</p>\n<p>You earned <em>%s" +
        " frequent renter points</em></p>",
        customers[i],
        rentalInfo(
          "<p>", "</p>",
          customers[i].getRentals())),
      customers[i].htmlStatement());
  }
}

@Test
(expected=IllegalArgumentException.class)
public void invalidTitle() {
  ObjectMother
    .customerWithNoRentals("Bob")
    .addRental(
      new Rental(
        new Movie("Crazy, Stupid, Love.",
                  Movie.Type.UNKNOWN),
        4));
}
```

```
public static String rentalInfo(
  String startsWith,
  String endsWith,
  List<Rental> rentals) {
  String result = "";
  for (Rental rental : rentals)
    result += String.format(
      "%s%s\t%s%s\n",
      startsWith,
      rental.getMovie().getTitle(),
      rental.getCharge(),
      endsWith);
  return result;
}

public static String expStatement(
  String formatStr,
  Customer customer,
  String rentalInfo) {
  return String.format(
    formatStr,
    customer.getName(),
    rentalInfo,
    customer.getTotalCharge(),
    customer.getTotalPoints());
}
}
```

Final

```
public class CustomerTest {
  @Test
  public void getName() {
    assertEquals(
      "John",
      a.customer.w(
        "John").build().getName());
  }

  @Test
  public void noRentalsStatement() {
    assertEquals(
      "Rental record for David\nAmount " +
      "owed is 0.0\nYou earned 0 frequent " +
      "renter points",
      a.customer.w(
        "David").build().statement());
  }
```

```java
@Test
public void oneNewReleaseStatement() {
  assertEquals(
    "Rental record for John\n" +
    "\tGodfather 4 9.0\n" +
    "Amount owed is 9.0\n" +
    "You earned 2 frequent renter points",
    a.customer.w("John").w(
      a.rental.w(
        a.movie.w(
          NEW_RELEASE))).build()
    .statement());
}

@Test
public void allRentalTypesStatement() {
  assertEquals(
    "Rental record for Pat\n" +
    "\tGodfather 4 9.0\n" +
    "\tScarface 3.5\n" +
    "\tLion King 1.5\n" +
    "Amount owed is 14.0\n" +
    "You earned 4 frequent renter points",
    a.customer.w("Pat").w(
      a.rental.w(a.movie.w(NEW_RELEASE)),
      a.rental.w(
        a.movie.w("Scarface").w(REGULAR)),
      a.rental.w(
        a.movie.w("Lion King").w(
          CHILDREN))).build().statement());
}
```

```
@Test
public void
newReleaseAndRegularStatement() {
  assertEquals(
    "Rental record for Steve\n" +
    "\tGodfather 4 9.0\n" +
    "\tScarface 3.5\n" +
    "Amount owed is 12.5\n" +
    "You earned 3 frequent renter points",
    a.customer.w("Steve").w(
      a.rental.w(a.movie.w(NEW_RELEASE)),
      a.rental.w(
        a.movie.w("Scarface").w(
          REGULAR))).build().statement());
}


@Test
public void noRentalsHtmlStatement() {
  assertEquals(
    "<h1>Rental record for <em>David" +
    "</em></h1>\n<p>Amount owed is <em>" +
    "0.0</em></p>\n<p>You earned <em>0 " +
    "frequent renter points</em></p>",
    a.customer.w(
      "David").build().htmlStatement());
}
```

```
@Test
public void oneNewReleaseHtmlStatement() {
  assertEquals(
    "<h1>Rental record for <em>John</em>" +
    "</h1>\n<p>Godfather 4 9.0</p>\n" +
    "<p>Amount owed is <em>9.0</em></p>" +
    "\n<p>You earned <em>2 frequent " +
    "renter points</em></p>",
    a.customer.w("John").w(
      a.rental.w(
        a.movie.w(
          NEW_RELEASE))).build()
    .htmlStatement());
}
```

```
@Test
public void allRentalTypesHtmlStatement() {
  assertEquals(
    "<h1>Rental record for <em>Pat</em>" +
    "</h1>\n<p>Godfather 4 9.0</p>\n" +
    "<p>Scarface 3.5</p>\n<p>Lion King" +
    " 1.5</p>\n<p>Amount owed is <em>" +
    "14.0</em></p>\n<p>You earned <em>" +
    "4 frequent renter points</em></p>",
    a.customer.w("Pat").w(
      a.rental.w(a.movie.w(NEW_RELEASE)),
      a.rental.w(
        a.movie.w("Scarface").w(REGULAR)),
      a.rental.w(
        a.movie.w("Lion King").w(
          CHILDREN))).build()
    .htmlStatement());
}
```

```
@Test
public void
newReleaseAndRegularHtmlStatement() {
  assertEquals(
    "<h1>Rental record for <em>Steve" +
    "</em></h1>\n<p>Godfather 4 9.0</p>" +
    "\n<p>Scarface 3.5</p>\n<p>Amount " +
    "owed is <em>12.5</em></p>\n<p>" +
    "You earned <em>3 frequent renter " +
    "points</em></p>",
    a.customer.w("Steve").w(
      a.rental.w(a.movie.w(NEW_RELEASE)),
      a.rental.w(
        a.movie.w("Scarface").w(
          REGULAR))).build()
    .htmlStatement());
}


@Test
(expected=IllegalArgumentException.class)
public void invalidTitle() {
  a.customer.w(
    a.rental.w(
      a.movie.w(UNKNOWN))).build();
  }
}
```

Final Thoughts on our Tests

The tests in this chapter are fairly simple, and yet they still provide more than enough content to create discussion among most software engineers.

Whether you prefer the original or final versions of `CustomerTest`, it's undeniable that the final version creates far tinier universes to work within. At this point you should have a fairly deep understanding of this simple example. That hard won deep understanding can be misleading when assessing the relative merits of the two testing approaches. If you write tests assuming the same level of understanding, you force future maintainers to gain that understanding. Conversely, the tests from the final example put all of the test data either directly in the test or in what should be a globally understood class.

> The decision to write DRY or DAMP tests often comes down to whether or not you want to force future maintainers to deeply understand code written strictly for testing purposes.

An interesting side note: despite replacing DRY tests with DAMP tests, the overall number of lines in the `CustomerTest` class barely changed.

The 'Final' version of CustomerTest improved in a few subtle ways that weren't previously emphasized.

- A test that contains more than one assertion (or one assertion that lives in a loop) will terminate on the first failure. By breaking the iteration into individual tests we were able to see all of the failures generated by our domain code change.
- The invalidTitle test uses the same instance creation code that all of the other Customer tests use. Now that all Customer, Rental, and Movie instances are created by a DataBuilder you can make constructor argument changes and the only consequence will be making a change to the build method for the associated *Builder class.

If you're with me this far, it should be relatively clear what a DAMP test is, and that I believe them to be far more valuable than DRY tests. From here we'll drop a bit into theory, then straight into deeper examples of how to evolve your tests towards a DAMP style, and finally we'll finish with test suite level improvements and what to avoid once you venture on to *Broad Stack Tests*.

Motivators

There are many ways to succeed while writing tests; however, let's start with an example of the more common path.

Let's imagine you read Unit Testing Tips: Write Maintainable Unit Tests That Will Save You Time And Tears[6] and decide that Roy Osherove has shown you the light. You're going to write all your tests with Roy's suggestions in mind. You get the entire team to read Roy's article and everyone adopts the patterns.

Things are going well until you start accidentally breaking tests that someone else wrote and you can't figure out why. It turns out that some object created in the Setup method is causing unexpected failures due to a side-effect of your 'minor' change. You're frustrated, having been burned by Setup, and you remember the blog entry by Jim Newkirk where he discussed Why you should not use SetUp and TearDown in NUnit[7]. Now you're stuck with a Setup heavy test suite, and a growing suspicion that you've gone down the wrong path.

You do more research on Setup and stumble upon Inline Setup. You can entirely relate and go on a mission to switch all the tests to xUnit.net; xUnit.net removes the concept of Setup entirely.

Everything looks good initially, but then a few constructors start needing more dependencies. Every test creates an in-

---

[6] http://msdn.microsoft.com/en-us/magazine/cc163665.aspx

[7] http://jamesnewkirk.typepad.com/posts/2007/09/why-you-should-.html

stance of an object; you moved the object creation out of the Setup and into each individual test. So now every test that creates that object needs to be updated. It becomes painful every time you add an argument to a constructor. You're once again left feeling like you've been burnt by following "expert" advice.

The root problem: you never asked yourself 'why?'. Why are you writing tests in the first place? Each testing practice you've chosen, what motivated you to adopt it?

You won't write better software by **blindly** following advice. This is especially true given that much of the advice around testing is inconsistent or outright conflicting. While I'm writing this chapter there's currently a twitter discussion with Martin Fowler, Michael Feathers, Bob Martin, Prag Dave, and David Heinemeier Hansson (all well respected and successful software engineers) where there are drastically conflicting opinions on how to effectively test. If there's a universally right way, we haven't found it yet.

> It's worth noting that the articles from Roy and Jim are quite old. Roy has since changed his mind on Setup (his current opinions can be found at artofunittesting.com), and I'm sure Jim has updated his opinions as well. The point of the example is to show how it's easy to blindly follow advice that sounds good, not to tie a good or bad idea with an individual.

Back to our painful journey above: your intentions were good. You want to write better software, so you followed some reasonable advice. Unfortunately, the advice you've chosen to follow left you with more pain than happiness. Your tests aren't providing enough value to justify their effort and if you keep going down this path you'll inevitably conclude that testing is stupid and it should be abandoned.

If you've traveled the path above or if you aren't regularly writing unit tests, you may find yourself wondering why other developers find them so essential. Ultimately I believe the answer boils down to selecting testing patterns based on what's motivating you to test.

The remainder of this chapter will focus on defining testing motivators. The list that follows is presented unordered, and includes both helpful and harmful motivators. Neither inclusion nor list index reflect the value of a motivator.

Validate the System

Common motivators that would be a subset of Validate the System

- Immediate Feedback That Things Work as Expected
- Prevent Future Regressions

Static languages like Java provide a compiler that protects you from a certain class of errors; however, unit tests often prove their value when you need to verify not the type of a result, but the value of the result. For example, if your shopping cart cannot correctly calculate the total of each contained item, it won't really matter that the result is an Integer.

For this reason, every codebase would benefit from, if nothing else, wrapping a few unit tests around the features of the system that if broken would cause the system to become unusable.

Theoretically, you could write a test to validate every feature of your system; however, I believe you would quickly find this task to be substantial and not necessarily worth your time - certain features of your system will likely be more important than others.

There's a common term in finance: ROI

> Return on investment (ROI) is the concept of an investment of some resource yielding a benefit to the investor. A high ROI means the investment gains compare favorably to investment cost.

When I'm motivated to write a test to validate the system, I like to look at the test from an ROI point of view. My favorite example for demonstrating how I choose based on ROI is the following:

Given a system where customers are looked up exclusively by Social Security Number

- I would unit test that a Social Security Number is valid at account creation time
- I would not unit test that a user's name is alpha-numeric.

Losing a new account based on an invalid Social Security Number could be rather harmful to a business; however, storing an incorrect name for a limited amount of time should have no impact on successful use of the system.

As long as everyone on the team understands the ROI of the various features, you could trust everyone to make the right call on when and when not to test based on ROI. If your team cannot reasonably grant that responsibility and power to each team member then it will likely make sense to either pair program or err on the side of over testing and evaluating the ROI of each test during a code review.

Tests written to validate the system are often used both to verify that the system currently works as expected as well as to prevent future regression.

Code Coverage

Automated code coverage metrics can be a wonderful thing when used correctly. Upon joining a project I often use code coverage to get a feel for the level of quality that I can expect from the application code. A low coverage percentage can show probable lack of quality - though I would consider it more of a hint than a guarantee. A high coverage percentage would make me feel better about the likelihood of finding a well designed codebase, but that's also more of a hint than a guarantee.

> I expect a high level of coverage. Sometimes managers require one. There's a subtle difference.
> –Brian Marick

I tend to agree with Martin Fowler's view on the subject: *If you are testing thoughtfully and well, I would expect a coverage percentage in the upper 80s or 90s. I would be suspicious of anything like 100% - it would smell of someone writing tests to make the coverage numbers happy, but not thinking about what they are doing.*

Once upon a time a consultancy went as far as putting "100% code coverage" in their contracts. It was a noble goal; unfortunately, a few years later the same consultancy was presenting on the topic of: How to fail with 100% test coverage. There are various problems with pushing towards 100%:

- You'll have to test language features.
- You'll have to test framework features.
- You'll have to maintain a lot of tests with negative ROI.
- etcetera

> I find that code coverage metrics over time may signal an interesting change that you may have otherwise missed, but as an absolute number, it's not very useful. –John Hume

> My favorite "100% code coverage" story involves a team that added a bunch of tests to get to 100%... but didn't add any assertions. Code coverage and verification are not the same thing. –Kent Spillner

I suspect most projects will suffer from the opposite, *not enough coverage.* The good news is it's quite simple to run a coverage tool and determine which pieces of code are untested.

I've had success using EMMA and Clover, and John Hume recently pointed me to Cobertura. Code coverage tools are easy to work with; there's no reason you couldn't try a few and decide which you prefer.

Again, code coverage tools are great. I personally strive for around 80% coverage. If you're looking to get above 80%, it would not surprise me to find tests that have code-coverage as their lone motivator.

Enable Refactoring

Getting test coverage on an untested codebase is always painful; however, it's also essential if you're planning to make any changes within the codebase. With the proper tests in place, you should be able to rewrite the internals of a codebase without breaking any of the existing contracts.

In addition to helping you prevent regression, creating tests can also give you direction on where the application can be logically broken up. While writing tests for a codebase you should keep track of dependencies that need to be instantiated, mocked or stubbed but have nothing to do with the current functionality you are focusing on. In general, these are the pieces that should be broken into components that are easily stubbed (ideally in 1 or 0 lines).

Document the Behavior of the System

When encountering a codebase for the first time, some developers go straight to the tests. These developers read the tests, test names as well as method bodies, to determine the how and why the system works as it does. These same developers enjoy the benefits of automated tests, but they value the documentation of tests almost as much or more than the functional aspect of the tests.

It's absolutely true that the code doesn't lie, and both correct and incorrect comments (including test names) can often give a view into what a developer was thinking when the test was written. If developers use tests as documentation, it's only natural that they create many tests, some of which would likely be unnecessary if they didn't exist solely to document the system.

Before you go deleting what appear to be superfluous tests, make sure you don't have someone on the team that sees your worthless test as essential documentation.

Your Manager Told You To

If this were your only motivator for writing a test, I think you'd be in a very paradoxical position. If you write worthless tests you're sure to anger your manager. Given that you're forced to write "meaningful" tests, I believe you'd want to write the most maintainable tests possible despite your lack of additional motivators. I imagine that you'll want to spend as little time as possible reading and writing tests, and the only way I see accomplishing that is by focusing on maintainability.

Thus, even if you don't particularly value testing, it will likely benefit you to seek out the most maintainable way to write tests in your context.

Test Driven Development

Common motivators that would be a subset of TDD

- Breaking a Problem up into Smaller Pieces

- Defining the "Simplest Thing that Could Possibly Work"
- Improved Design

Unit Testing and TDD are often incorrectly conflated and referred to by either name. Unit testing is an umbrella name for testing at a certain level of abstraction. TDD has a very specific definition:

> Test-driven development (TDD) is a software development process that relies on the repetition of a very short development cycle: first the developer writes an (initially failing) automated test case that defines a desired improvement or new function, then produces the minimum amount of code to pass that test, and finally refactors the new code to acceptable standards. –Wikipedia

It's not necessary to write unit tests to TDD, nor is it necessary to TDD to write unit tests.

That said, there's a reason that the terms are often conflated: If you're practicing TDD, then you're very likely also writing a substantial amount of unit tests. A codebase written by developers dogmatically following TDD would theoretically contain no code that wasn't written as a result of a failing test. Proponents of TDD often claim that the results of TDD give the existing team and future maintainers a greater level of confidence.

TDD's development cycle is also very appealing to developers who can find a large problem overwhelming, but are able to quickly break a large problem down into many smaller tests that, when combined, solve the larger problem. Rather than focusing on the single large problem and trying to write code that solves for every known problem, the developers will focus on writing tests for each individual variable and growing the code in a way where each test keeps passing and each variable is dealt with individually.

Incredibly large and complicated problems don't seem nearly as daunting when programmers are able to focus exclusively on the task at hand: **make the individual test pass**. In addition, all of the previously written tests provide a safety net, thus allowing you to (harmlessly) ignore all prior constraints.

Proponents of TDD generally believe it promotes superior design as well. Two reasons are the most often used when describing the design benefits of TDD:

- By focusing on the test cases first, a developer is forced to imagine how the functionality will be used by clients.
- TDD leads to more modularized, flexible, and extensible code by requiring that the developers think of the software in terms of small units that can be written and tested independently and integrated together later.

In my opinion every developer should practice TDD at some point in their career. Utilizing TDD at the right moment will unquestionably make you more productive. That said, the frequency of those moments often depends greatly on the individual. Only through experience can a developer know how to judge whether the current moment would benefit or suffer from switching to a TDD cycle.

An anonymous comment once appeared on my blog:

> The developers that know how to write tests correctly are very rare, and only those developers

can really do TDD. The rest end up with a nest of poorly written brittle tests that don't fully test the code.

It's my hope that this book will help increase the number of developers that are productively unit testing. Still, it's perfectly reasonable to delete a test that provided value as part of a TDD cycle, but no longer has positive ROI.

Customer Acceptance

Unit Testing to achieve customer acceptance would be an interesting choice. Rarely would a domain expert be willing to sift through all of the unit tests to determine whether or not they're willing to sign off on the system. Thus, I imagine you'd need to devise some type of filtering that allowed the domain expert to drill down to what they believed to be important.

My default choice is to enable the domain expert to write and maintain tests in a tool designed for high level tests; removing developers and unit tests almost entirely from the acceptance process. However, if the developers must be responsible for writing the tests used for customer acceptance, I would devise a plan to annotate the appropriate unit tests and provide a well formatted report based on the automated results.

In my experience, developers are willing to support customer acceptance low level tests that can quickly be debugged when they fail. Conversely, I've never seen a developer that was happy to maintain tests that are both strictly for the customer and high level (thus hard to debug).

Ping Pong Pair-Programming

From the c2.com Wiki

> here's how Pair Programming works on my team.
>
> 1. A writes a new test and sees that it fails.
> 2. B implements the code needed to pass the test.
> 3. B writes the next test and sees that it fails.
> 4. A implements the code needed to pass the test.
>
> And so on.

While the most popular definition obviously describes a TDD approach, there's no reason you couldn't ping-pong writing the test after. If you're already pair programming, the rhythm created by practicing ping-pong may be the only motivator you need for writing a test. I've seen this approach utilized very successfully.

Once a feature is complete it's often worth your time to examine the associated tests. Many of the recently created tests will be valuable as is. Other tests may provide negative ROI as written, but with small tweaks can be made to produce positive ROI. Finally, any tests that were motivated solely by the development process should be considered for deletion.

What Motivates You (or Your Team)

The primary driver for this chapter is to recognize that tests can be written for many different reasons, and assuming that a test is necessary simply because it exists is not always the right decision. It's valuable to recognize which motivators are responsible for a test that you're creating or updating. If you come across a test with no motivators, do everyone a favor and delete the test.

I often write speculative tests that help me get to feature completion, but are unnecessary in the long term. Those are the tests that I look to delete once a feature is complete. They're valuable to me for brainstorming purposes, but aren't well designed for documentation, regression detection, or any other motivator. Once they've served their purpose, I happily kill them off.

Deleting tests that no longer provide value is an important activity; however, deleting tests is an activity that shouldn't be taken lightly. Each test deletion likely requires at least a little collaboration to ensure that (as I previously mentioned) your valueless test isn't someone else's documentation.

Types of Tests

Before we get back to concrete examples there are a few terms we'll want to define: *State Verification, Behavior Verification, Solitary Unit Test,* and *Sociable Unit Test.*

Strongly Recommended Reference Material

In the next few sections I'll put some basic definitions around state and behavior verification. If you're looking for additional material on this subject, I would highly recommend reading Mocks Aren't Stubs[8] for a well written, in-depth explanation of mocks, stubs, and their impact on testing.

---

[8]http://www.martinfowler.com/articles/mocksArentStubs.html

State Verification

State Verification describes a style of testing where you exercise one or many methods of an object and then assert the expected state of the object (and/or collaborators). In *Mocks Aren't Stubs* Martin Fowler identifies developers who generally rely on state verification as *Classicists*. The primary argument for a *Classicists'* style might be stated as: State verification tests specify the least possible implementation detail, thus they will continue to pass even if the internals of the methods being tested are changed.

As long as the external interface remains unchanged, the following state verification tests should continue to pass regardless of modification to the internals of `Rental` and `Store`.

> note: The following `RentalBuilder` and `StoreBuilder` instances use a (previously undocumented) `w` method that takes a `Movie` instance. When using the *DataBuilder* pattern it's very common to have an overloaded `w` method that takes either the builder or an instance of the class.

```
public class RentalTest {
  @Test
  public void rentalIsStartedIfInStore() {
    Movie movie = a.movie.build();
    Rental rental =
      a.rental.w(movie).build();
    Store store = a.store.w(movie).build();
    rental.start(store);
    assertTrue(rental.isStarted());
    assertEquals(
      0, store.getAvailability(movie));
  }

  @Test
  public void
  rentalDoesNotStartIfNotAvailable() {
    Movie movie = a.movie.build();
    Rental rental = a.rental.build();
    Store store = a.store.build();
    rental.start(store);
    assertFalse(rental.isStarted());
    assertEquals(
      0, store.getAvailability(movie));
  }
}
```

In the test above we're verifying the started state of Rental; however, it's not possible to test a Rental without a Store as well. The Rental would be considered the Subject Under Test (SUT) as defined in Martin's previously referenced *Mocks Aren't Stubs*; however, I prefer the term Class Under Test (for reasons later described). In the RentalTest the Store instance is merely a collaborator.

State verification tests generally rely on assertions to verify the state of our objects; in our example we assert the state of `rental.isStarted()` and `store.getAvailability(movie)`.

> note: The Classicist/Mockist dichotomy is about more than testing, but the additional details are outside the scope of this book. More information can be found in the previously linked *Mocks Aren't Stubs* article.

Behavior Verification

Behavior Verification describes a style of testing where the execution of a method is expected to generate specific interactions between objects. In *Mocks Aren't Stubs* Martin Fowler describes developers who generally rely on behavior verification as *Mockists*. Behavior verification is about specifying how the system should behave as it operates rather than specifying the expected end state of the system after it has completed an operation.

One common criticism of the behavior verification approach is that implementation changes that preserve macro behavior can lead to difficult to understand and largely valueless test failures. Unsurprisingly, *Mockists* have developed a style of test development that helps avoid this fragility.

Behavior verification tests with minimal collaborators can effectively verify interactions without sacrificing maintainability. As a result, a team that relies on Behavior verification will likely produce a codebase with few *Law of Demeter*[9] violations and a focus on *Tell, Don't Ask*[10].

> For those unfamiliar with *Law of Demeter* and *Tell, Don't Ask*, the *Law of Demeter* can be defined as *Only talk to your immediate friends* and *Tell, Don't Ask* can be defined as *Rather than asking an object for data and acting on that data, we should instead tell an object what to do.*

The following test verifies the interaction between a Rental and a Store.

---

[9]http://en.wikipedia.org/wiki/Law_of_Demeter
[10]http://martinfowler.com/bliki/TellDontAsk.html

```
public class RentalTest {
  @Test
  public void rentalIsStartedIfInStore() {
    Movie movie = a.movie.build();
    Rental rental =
      a.rental.w(movie).build();
    Store store = mock(Store.class);
    when(store.getAvailability(movie))
      .thenReturn(1);
    rental.start(store);
    assertTrue(rental.isStarted());
    verify(store).remove(movie);
  }

  @Test
  public void
  rentalDoesNotStartIfNotAvailable() {
    Rental rental = a.rental.build();
    Store store = mock(Store.class);
    rental.start(store);
    assertFalse(rental.isStarted());
    verify(
      store, never()).remove(
        any(Movie.class));
  }
}
```

In the test above we're verifying the Rental using state verification; however, we've switched to behavior verification for the Store collaborator. In our examples we're using the Mockito mocking framework to handle verification. Mockito mocks follow the pattern of create, (optionally) stub, verify. In our tests we create our mocks using the static method mock. In the first test we stub the result of `store.getAvailability`, in the second test no stubbing is necessary. Finally, both tests use the static method `verify` to assert the interactions the `Store` instance received during test execution.

The use of mock verification to ensure a system behaves as expected is a hallmark of the behavior verification approach to testing.

My examples have focused on behavior verification implemented with mocks, as that's how I tend to do behavior verification. While I don't use them in practice, for completeness I'll mention that spies[11] are another popular implementation of behavior verification.

Picking a Side

In *Mocks Aren't Stubs* Martin Fowler asks and answers the following:

> So should I be a classicist or a mockist? I find this
> a difficult question to answer with confidence.

If you've done much unit testing, it's likely that you already have a preference. If you haven't, you may find yourself leaning more toward one approach than the other. Personally, I've never been satisfied with the results from following the advice from either camp. As the book continues we'll explore my favorite approach, which is more of a hybrid, but for now the definitions above will suffice.

---

[11]http://xunitpatterns.com/Test%20Spy.html

Unit Test

The definition of Unit Test is quite general:

> In computer programming, unit testing is a method
> by which individual units of source code, sets of
> one or more computer program modules together
> with associated control data, usage procedures,
> and operating procedures are tested to determine
> if they are fit for use. [...] A unit could be an
> entire module, but it is more commonly an in-
> dividual function or procedure. –Wikipedia

The above definition states that a unit can be an individual
Java method, but it can also be something much larger that
likely includes many collaborating classes. I find value in
splitting my unit tests into two distinct categories - *Solitary
Unit Tests* and *Sociable Unit Tests*.

Solitary Unit Test

In Java it's common to unit test at the class level. The Foo class will have an associated FooTests class. *Solitary Unit Tests* follow two additional constraints:

1. Never cross boundaries
2. The Class Under Test should be the only concrete class found in a test.

Never cross boundaries is a fairly simple, yet controversial piece of advice. In 2004, Bill Caputo wrote about this advice, and defined a boundary as: *"...a database, a queue, another system..."*. The advice to avoid crossing these types of boundaries is grounded in performance concerns: accessing a database, network, or file system significantly increases the time it takes to run a test. When the aggregate execution time impacts a developer's decision to run the test suite, the effectiveness of the entire team is at risk. A test suite that isn't run regularly doesn't have many opportunities to provide positive ROI.

In the same entry, Bill also defines a boundary as: *"... or even an ordinary class if that class is 'outside' the area your [sic] trying to work with or are responsible for"*. Bill's recommendation is a good one, but I find it a bit vague and prefer concrete advice on where to draw the line. My second constraint is a concrete (and admittedly restrictive) version of Bill's recommendation.

The concept of constraining a unit test such that 'the Class Under Test should be the only concrete class found in a test' sounds extreme, but it's actually not that drastic if you assume a few things.

- You're using a framework such as Mockito that allows you to easily stub most concrete classes
- This constraint does not apply to any primitive or Java class that has a literal (e.g. int, Integer, String, etc)
- You're using some type of automated refactoring tool.

There are pros and cons to this approach, both of which we'll discuss later in the book. For now we will limit our focus to achieving a clear understanding of what a *Solitary Unit Test* is.

I define *Solitary Unit Test* as:

> Solitary Unit Testing is an activity by which methods of a class or functions of a namespace are tested to determine if they are fit for use. The tests used to determine if a class or namespace is functional should isolate the class or namespace under test by stubbing all collaboration with additional classes and namespaces.

Sociable Unit Test

The definition of *Sociable Unit Test* is simple: Any Unit Test that cannot be classified as a *Solitary Unit Test* is a *Sociable Unit Test*.

Continuing with Examples From Chapter 1

If you find yourself thinking, *"Given those definitions, we haven't seen a single Solitary Unit Test in this book"*, you're absolutely right. The very last (Behavior Verification) test we saw came close; however, it relies on a `RentalBuilder`, which creates a default instance of `Movie`.

It would have been possible to convert the tests in the first chapter to *Solitary Unit Tests*, but that would have required hand-rolling our own stubs or introducing a mocking framework. Hand-rolling your own stubs isn't something I generally recommend. Introducing a mocking framework would have been possible, but I didn't want the first chapter to overwhelm and drag-on endlessly. Instead, we ended Chapter 1 with vastly improved, yet still *Sociable Unit Tests*.

However, I do believe a good mix of *Solitary* and *Sociable Unit Tests* tests is a superior solution, and now feels like a good time to create some concrete examples of *Solitary Unit Tests*.

Let's revisit the last `CustomerTest` we saw in Chapter 1.

```java
public class CustomerTest {
  @Test
  public void getName() {
    assertEquals(
      "John",
      a.customer.w(
        "John").build().getName());
  }


  @Test
  public void noRentalsStatement() {
    assertEquals(
      "Rental record for David\nAmount" +
      " owed is 0.0\n" +
      "You earned 0 frequent renter points",
      a.customer.w(
        "David").build().statement());
  }


  @Test
  public void oneNewReleaseStatement() {
    assertEquals(
      "Rental record for John\n" +
      "\tGodfather 4 9.0\n" +
      "Amount owed is 9.0\n" +
      "You earned 2 frequent renter points",
      a.customer.w("John").w(
        a.rental.w(
          a.movie.w(
            NEW_RELEASE))).build()
      .statement());
  }
```

```
@Test
public void allRentalTypesStatement() {
  assertEquals(
    "Rental record for Pat\n" +
    "\tGodfather 4 9.0\n" +
    "\tScarface 3.5\n" +
    "\tLion King 1.5\n" +
    "Amount owed is 14.0\n" +
    "You earned 4 frequent renter points",
    a.customer.w("Pat").w(
      a.rental.w(a.movie.w(NEW_RELEASE)),
      a.rental.w(
        a.movie.w("Scarface").w(REGULAR)),
      a.rental.w(
        a.movie.w(
          "Lion King").w(
            CHILDREN))).build()
    .statement());
}
```

```
@Test
public void
newReleaseAndRegularStatement() {
  assertEquals(
    "Rental record for Steve\n" +
    "\tGodfather 4 9.0\n" +
    "\tScarface 3.5\n" +
    "Amount owed is 12.5\n" +
    "You earned 3 frequent renter points",
    a.customer.w("Steve").w(
      a.rental.w(a.movie.w(NEW_RELEASE)),
      a.rental.w(
        a.movie.w("Scarface").w(
          REGULAR))).build()
    .statement());
}


@Test
public void noRentalsHtmlStatement() {
  assertEquals(
    "<h1>Rental record for <em>David" +
    "</em></h1>\n<p>Amount owed is " +
    "<em>0.0</em></p>\n<p>" +
    "You earned <em>0 frequent renter " +
    "points</em></p>",
    a.customer.w(
      "David").build().htmlStatement());
}
```

```
@Test
public void oneNewReleaseHtmlStatement() {
  assertEquals(
    "<h1>Rental record for <em>John</em>" +
    "</h1>\n<p>Godfather 4 9.0</p>\n" +
    "<p>Amount owed is <em>9.0</em></p>" +
    "\n<p>You earned <em>2 frequent " +
    "renter points</em></p>",
    a.customer.w("John").w(
      a.rental.w(
        a.movie.w(NEW_RELEASE))).build()
    .htmlStatement());
}


@Test
public void allRentalTypesHtmlStatement() {
  assertEquals(
    "<h1>Rental record for <em>Pat</em>" +
    "</h1>\n<p>Godfather 4 9.0</p>\n<p>" +
    "Scarface 3.5</p>\n<p>Lion King 1.5" +
    "</p>\n<p>Amount owed is <em>14.0" +
    "</em></p>\n<p>You earned <em>4 " +
    "frequent renter points</em></p>",
    a.customer.w("Pat").w(
      a.rental.w(a.movie.w(NEW_RELEASE)),
      a.rental.w(a.movie.w("Scarface").w(
                 REGULAR)),
      a.rental.w(a.movie.w("Lion King").w(
                 CHILDREN))).build()
    .htmlStatement());
}
```

```
@Test
public void
newReleaseAndRegularHtmlStatement() {
  assertEquals(
    "<h1>Rental record for <em>Steve" +
    "</em></h1>\n<p>Godfather 4 9.0</p>" +
    "\n<p>Scarface 3.5</p>\n<p>Amount " +
    "owed is <em>12.5</em></p>\n<p>You " +
    "earned <em>3 frequent renter points" +
    "</em></p>",
    a.customer.w("Steve").w(
      a.rental.w(a.movie.w(NEW_RELEASE)),
      a.rental.w(a.movie.w("Scarface").w(
                  REGULAR))).build()
    .htmlStatement());
}


@Test
(expected=IllegalArgumentException.class)
public void invalidTitle() {
  a.customer.w(
    a.rental.w(
      a.movie.w(UNKNOWN))).build();
  }
}
```

CustomerTest is entirely too long and too fragile. These tests are somewhat tiny universes with literal expected values, but those values are often too long to easily digest and many of these universes include several different concrete classes.

As I previously mentioned, were this my codebase, the first thing I would look to do is create more fine-grained tests.

The `invalidTitle()` test is an obvious candidate. There's no reason to test this exception in `CustomerTest`.

```
public class MovieTest {
  @Test
  (expected=IllegalArgumentException.class)
  public void invalidTitle() {
    a.movie.w(UNKNOWN).build();
  }
}
```

The newly introduced `MovieTest` is our first true *Solitary Unit Test*, and it's a good one. The `invalidTitle` tiny universe crosses no boundaries, so it's incredibly fast; it also requires no collaborators, thus only changes to `Movie` will cause this test to fail.

Back in the `CustomerTest` it's time to address something that's been bothering me for almost 40 pages: our `statement` and `htmlStatement` tests are conflating verification of summing, string building, `Movie` points, and `Movie` charges. It's time to break those into individual tests.

When it comes to string building I'm all for testing a customer with 0, 1, & 2 rentals, and one way to concisely test those scenarios is to switch to using stubs.

```java
public class CustomerTest {
  @Test
  public void noRentalsStatement() {
    assertEquals(
      "Rental record for Jim\nAmount owed" +
      " is 0.0\n" +
      "You earned 0 frequent renter points",
      a.customer.build().statement());
  }

  @Test
  public void oneRentalStatement() {
    assertEquals(
      "Rental record for Jim\n\tnull\n" +
      "Amount owed is 0.0\n" +
      "You earned 0 frequent renter points",
      a.customer.w(
        mock(Rental.class)).build()
      .statement());
  }
```

```
@Test
public void twoRentalsStatement() {
  assertEquals(
    "Rental record for Jim\n\t" +
    "null\n\tnull\n" +
    "Amount owed is 0.0\n" +
    "You earned 0 frequent renter points",
    a.customer.w(
      mock(Rental.class),
      mock(Rental.class)).build()
    .statement());
  }
}
```

The switch to stub collaborators leaves the tests above much more concise, but they do leave a bit to be desired. The first time you encounter null values within an expected value you may wonder if you've discovered a mistake. Additionally, we've lost the verification of point and charge summing.

The Rental stubs could be altered to return non-null values to concatenate. Personally, I find adding code to change the String *"null"* to some other magic String is a negative ROI activity. I prefer to accept null as the default String return value, and avoid any need for method stubbing. The expected values become easy to digest once you internalize and embrace null as a default return value.

You might have also noticed that I switched each name to *"Jim"*. You could argue that I should specify the name in the test if I'm going to use it in my expected string. In theory I agree this is a good guideline. In practice, the defaults should never change. With that in mind, I generally prefer to opt for relying on a default and writing shorter tests.

The (now required) point and charge summing tests can be seen below.

```
public class CustomerTest {
  @Test
  public void noRentalsCharge() {
    assertEquals(
      0.0,
      a.customer.build().getTotalCharge(),
      0);
  }

  @Test
  public void twoRentalsCharge() {
    Rental rental = mock(Rental.class);
    when(rental.getCharge()).thenReturn(2.0);
    assertEquals(
      4.0,
      a.customer.w(
        rental,
        rental).build().getTotalCharge(),
      0);
  }
}
```

```
@Test
public void threeRentalsCharge() {
  Rental rental = mock(Rental.class);
  when(rental.getCharge()).thenReturn(2.0);
  assertEquals(
    6.0,
    a.customer.w(
      rental,
      rental,
      rental).build().getTotalCharge(),
    0);
}

@Test
public void noRentalsPoints() {
  assertEquals(
    0,
    a.customer.build().getTotalPoints());
}

@Test
public void twoRentalsPoints() {
  Rental rental = mock(Rental.class);
  when(rental.getPoints()).thenReturn(2);
  assertEquals(
    4,
    a.customer.w(
      rental,
      rental).build().getTotalPoints());
}
```

```
@Test
public void threeRentalsPoints() {
  Rental rental = mock(Rental.class);
  when(rental.getPoints()).thenReturn(2);
  assertEquals(
    6,
    a.customer.w(
      rental,
      rental,
      rental).build().getTotalPoints());
  }
}
```

With those tests in place it's time to add point and charge verification to our MovieTest class.

```
public class MovieTest {
  @Test
  public void getChargeForChildrens() {
    assertEquals(
      1.5,
      a.movie.w(
        CHILDREN).build().getCharge(1),
      0);
    assertEquals(
      1.5,
      a.movie.w(
        CHILDREN).build().getCharge(2),
      0);
    assertEquals(
      1.5,
      a.movie.w(
        CHILDREN).build().getCharge(3),
      0);
    assertEquals(
      3.0,
      a.movie.w(
        CHILDREN).build().getCharge(4),
      0);
    assertEquals(
      4.5,
      a.movie.w(
        CHILDREN).build().getCharge(5),
      0);
  }
```

```java
@Test
public void getChargeForNewRelease() {
  assertEquals(
    3.0,
    a.movie.w(
      NEW_RELEASE).build().getCharge(1),
    0);
  assertEquals(
    6.0,
    a.movie.w(
      NEW_RELEASE).build().getCharge(2),
    0);
  assertEquals(
    9.0,
    a.movie.w(
      NEW_RELEASE).build().getCharge(3),
    0);
}
```

```
@Test
public void getChargeForRegular() {
  assertEquals(
    2.0,
    a.movie.w(
      REGULAR).build().getCharge(1),
    0);
  assertEquals(
    2.0,
    a.movie.w(
      REGULAR).build().getCharge(2),
    0);
  assertEquals(
    3.5,
    a.movie.w(
      REGULAR).build().getCharge(3),
    0);
  assertEquals(
    5.0,
    a.movie.w(
      REGULAR).build().getCharge(4),
    0);
}
```

```
@Test
public void getPointsForChildrens() {
  assertEquals(
    1,
    a.movie.w(
      CHILDREN).build().getPoints(1));
  assertEquals(
    1,
    a.movie.w(
      CHILDREN).build().getPoints(2));
}

@Test
public void getPointsForNewRelease() {
  assertEquals(
    1,
    a.movie.w(
      NEW_RELEASE).build().getPoints(1));
  assertEquals(
    2,
    a.movie.w(
      NEW_RELEASE).build().getPoints(2));
  assertEquals(
    2,
    a.movie.w(
      NEW_RELEASE).build().getPoints(3));
}
```

```
@Test
public void getPointsForRegular() {
  assertEquals(
    1,
    a.movie.w(
      REGULAR).build().getPoints(1));
  assertEquals(
    1,
    a.movie.w(
      REGULAR).build().getPoints(2));
  }
}
```

These new fine-grained CustomerTest and MovieTest *Solitary Unit Tests* give me confidence in the system, and I also feel comfortable that changes to a given class will only create failures in the tests for the Class Under Test. For example, I do not believe that changes to Movie will cause a failure in CustomerTest.

Despite my happiness with these *Solitary Unit Tests*, there's still one more test I would write. Similar to my belief that a hybrid of State Verification and Behavior Verification is superior, I believe a combination of *Solitary* and *Sociable Unit Tests* will provide a greater ROI than selecting one exclusively.

The *Final Thoughts* CustomerTest from Chapter 1 contains fairly well written *Sociable Unit Tests*, my only real complaint is that it tries to cover code-paths that are more effectively covered with *Solitary Unit Tests* (as we've done above). Still, the following slimmed down version of CustomerTest serves as a very helpful *Sociable Unit Test*.

```java
public class CustomerTest {
  @Test
  public void allRentalTypesStatement() {
    assertEquals(
      "Rental record for Pat\n" +
      "\tGodfather 4 9.0\n" +
      "\tScarface 3.5\n" +
      "\tLion King 1.5\n" +
      "Amount owed is 14.0\n" +
      "You earned 4 frequent renter points",
      a.customer.w("Pat").w(
        a.rental.w(a.movie.w(NEW_RELEASE)),
        a.rental.w(a.movie.w("Scarface").w(
                    REGULAR)),
        a.rental.w(a.movie.w("Lion King").w(
                    CHILDREN)))
      .build().statement());
  }
```

```
@Test
public void allRentalTypesHtmlStatement() {
  assertEquals(
    "<h1>Rental record for " +
    "<em>Pat</em></h1>\n" +
    "<p>Godfather 4 9.0</p>\n" +
    "<p>Scarface 3.5</p>\n" +
    "<p>Lion King 1.5</p>\n" +
    "<p>Amount owed is " +
    "<em>14.0</em></p>\n<p>" +
    "You earned <em>4 frequent " +
    "renter points</em></p>",
    a.customer.w("Pat").w(
      a.rental.w(a.movie.w(NEW_RELEASE)),
      a.rental.w(a.movie.w("Scarface").w(
              REGULAR)),
      a.rental.w(a.movie.w("Lion King").w(
              CHILDREN)))
    .build().htmlStatement());
  }
}
```

The tests from the previous example provide positive ROI based on their verification of Customer, Rental, and Movie integrating successfully.

Despite their overall positive ROI, these tests have 2 potential issues:

- They run the risk of failing due to an implementation change in a collaborator.
- When they fail it can be hard to determine if the issue is coming from the Class Under Test, a collaborator, or somewhere else completely.

In practice I find you can keep the ROI positive if you mitigate the above issues with the following suggestions.

- Verify as much as you can with 1 happy path test per method. When things do go wrong, you want as little noise as possible. Limiting the number of *Sociable Unit Tests* can go a long way to helping the situation when things go wrong.
- If you stick to fixing the *Solitary Unit Tests* before the *Sociable Unit Tests*, by the time you get to a failing *Sociable Unit test* you should have a very good idea where to find the root of the problem.

Final Thoughts, Again

The *Solitary* and *Sociable Unit Tests* (up to this point) are provided below. It's not necessary that you read every line, but I think it's worth considering the tests in their entirety. We started with very complicated tests that were tough to rapidly digest. Making matters worse, we were stuck with a failing test and no simple path for finding the cause. The result we've refactored to is not only easier to quickly understand, but the same failure would be isolated to a significantly more focused test; thus, making it easier to diagnose and fix.

As I said, you don't need to read every line. Instead, I think it's valuable to try something similar to the exercise I provided in Chapter 1. Below you'll find the output from a failing test. If you're up for it, see if you can spot the issue in the code. Once you find the failure and the origin, consider that experience compared to the one you had in Chapter 1.

The Failure

```
JUnit version 4.11
..........E...
There was 1 failure:
1) twoRentalsCharge(solitary.CustomerTest)
java.lang.AssertionError: expected:<6.0> but was:\
<4.0>

FAILURES!!!
Tests run: 13,  Failures: 1
```

solitary.CustomerTest

```
public class CustomerTest {
  @Test
  public void getName() {
    assertEquals(
      "John",
      a.customer.w(
        "John").build().getName());
  }

  @Test
  public void noRentalsStatement() {
    assertEquals(
      "Rental record for Jim\nAmount owed" +
      " is 0.0\nYou earned 0 frequent " +
      "renter points",
      a.customer.build().statement());
  }

  @Test
  public void oneRentalStatement() {
    assertEquals(
      "Rental record for Jim\n\tnull\n" +
      "Amount owed is 0.0\n" +
      "You earned 0 frequent renter points",
      a.customer.w(
        mock(Rental.class)).build()
      .statement());
  }
}
```

```java
@Test
public void twoRentalsStatement() {
  assertEquals(
    "Rental record for Jim\n\n\tnull\n" +
    "\tnull\nAmount owed is 0.0\n" +
    "You earned 0 frequent renter points",
    a.customer.w(
      mock(Rental.class),
      mock(Rental.class)).build()
    .statement());
}


@Test
public void noRentalsHtmlStatement() {
  assertEquals(
    "<h1>Rental record for <em>Jim</em>" +
    "</h1>\n<p>Amount owed is <em>0.0" +
    "</em></p>\n<p>You earned <em>0 " +
    "frequent renter points</em></p>",
    a.customer.build().htmlStatement());
}
```

```java
@Test
public void oneRentalHtmlStatement() {
  Rental rental = mock(Rental.class);
  assertEquals(
    "<h1>Rental record for <em>Jim</em>" +
    "</h1>\n<p>null</p>\n<p>Amount owed " +
    "is <em>0.0</em></p>\n<p>You earned " +
    "<em>0 frequent renter points</em>" +
    "</p>",
    a.customer.w(
      mock(Rental.class)).build()
    .htmlStatement());
}

@Test
public void twoRentalsHtmlStatement() {
  assertEquals(
    "<h1>Rental record for <em>Jim</em>" +
    "</h1>\n<p>null</p>\n<p>null</p>\n" +
    "<p>Amount owed is <em>0.0</em></p>" +
    "\n<p>You earned <em>0 frequent" +
    " renter points</em></p>",
    a.customer.w(
      mock(Rental.class),
      mock(Rental.class)).build()
    .htmlStatement());
}
```

```
@Test
public void noRentalsCharge() {
  assertEquals(
    0.0,
    a.customer.build().getTotalCharge(),
    0);
}

@Test
public void twoRentalsCharge() {
  Rental rental = mock(Rental.class);
  when(rental.getCharge()).thenReturn(2.0);
  assertEquals(
    6.0,
    a.customer.w(
      rental,
      rental).build().getTotalCharge(),
    0);
}

@Test
public void threeRentalsCharge() {
  Rental rental = mock(Rental.class);
  when(rental.getCharge()).thenReturn(2.0);
  assertEquals(
    6.0,
    a.customer.w(
      rental,
      rental,
      rental).build().getTotalCharge(),
    0);
}
```

```
@Test
public void noRentalsPoints() {
  assertEquals(
    0,
    a.customer.build().getTotalPoints());
}

@Test
public void twoRentalsPoints() {
  Rental rental = mock(Rental.class);
  when(rental.getPoints()).thenReturn(2);
  assertEquals(
    4,
    a.customer.w(
      rental,
      rental).build().getTotalPoints());
}

@Test
public void threeRentalsPoints() {
  Rental rental = mock(Rental.class);
  when(rental.getPoints()).thenReturn(2);
  assertEquals(
    6,
    a.customer.w(
      rental,
      rental,
      rental).build().getTotalPoints());
  }
}
```

sociable.CustomerTest

```
public class CustomerTest {
  @Test
  public void allRentalTypesStatement() {
    assertEquals(
      "Rental record for Pat\n" +
      "\tGodfather 4 9.0\n" +
      "\tScarface 3.5\n" +
      "\tLion King 1.5\n" +
      "Amount owed is 14.0\n" +
      "You earned 4 frequent renter points",
      a.customer.w("Pat").w(
        a.rental.w(a.movie.w(NEW_RELEASE)),
        a.rental.w(a.movie.w("Scarface").w(
                    REGULAR)),
        a.rental.w(a.movie.w("Lion King").w(
                    CHILDREN)))
      .build().statement());
  }
```

```
@Test
public void allRentalTypesHtmlStatement() {
  assertEquals(
    "<h1>Rental record for <em>Pat" +
    "</em></h1>\n" +
    "<p>Godfather 4 9.0</p>\n" +
    "<p>Scarface 3.5</p>\n" +
    "<p>Lion King 1.5</p>\n" +
    "<p>Amount owed is " +
    "<em>14.0</em></p>\n<p>" +
    "You earned <em>4 " +
    "frequent renter points</em></p>",
    a.customer.w("Pat").w(
      a.rental.w(a.movie.w(NEW_RELEASE)),
      a.rental.w(a.movie.w("Scarface").w(
                  REGULAR)),
      a.rental.w(a.movie.w("Lion King").w(
                  CHILDREN)))
    .build().htmlStatement());
  }
}
```

Customer

```java
public class Customer {

  private String name;
  private List<Rental> rentals
  = new ArrayList<Rental>();

  public Customer(String name) {
    this.name = name;
  }

  public String getName() {
    return name;
  }

  public void addRental(Rental rental) {
    rentals.add(rental);
  }

  public String statement() {
    String result =
      "Rental record for " +
      getName() + "\n";
    for (Rental rental : rentals)
      result +=
        "\t" + rental.getLineItem() + "\n";
    result += "Amount owed is " +
      getTotalCharge() + "\n" +
      "You earned " + getTotalPoints() +
      " frequent renter points";
    return result;
  }
}
```

```
public String htmlStatement() {
  String result =
    "<h1>Rental record for <em>" +
    getName() + "</em></h1>\n";
  for (Rental rental : rentals)
    result +=
      "<p>" + rental.getLineItem() +
      "</p>\n";
  result +=
    "<p>Amount owed is <em>" +
    getTotalCharge() + "</em></p>\n" +
    "<p>You earned <em>" +
    getTotalPoints() +
    " frequent renter points</em></p>";
  return result;

}


public double getTotalCharge() {
  double total = 0;
  for (Rental rental : rentals)
    total += rental.getCharge();
  return total;
}

public int getTotalPoints() {
  int total = 0;
  for (Rental rental : rentals)
    total += rental.getPoints();
  return total;
}
}
```

solitary.MovieTest

```java
public class MovieTest {
  @Test
  public void getChargeForChildrens() {
    assertEquals(
      1.5,
      a.movie.w(
        CHILDREN).build().getCharge(1),
      0);
    assertEquals(
      1.5,
      a.movie.w(
        CHILDREN).build().getCharge(2),
      0);
    assertEquals(
      1.5,
      a.movie.w(
        CHILDREN).build().getCharge(3),
      0);
    assertEquals(
      3.0,
      a.movie.w(
        CHILDREN).build().getCharge(4),
      0);
    assertEquals(
      4.5,
      a.movie.w(
        CHILDREN).build().getCharge(5),
      0);
  }
```

```
@Test
public void getChargeForNewRelease() {
  assertEquals(
    3.0,
    a.movie.w(
      NEW_RELEASE).build().getCharge(1),
    0);
  assertEquals(
    6.0,
    a.movie.w(
      NEW_RELEASE).build().getCharge(2),
    0);
  assertEquals(
    9.0,
    a.movie.w(
      NEW_RELEASE).build().getCharge(3),
    0);
}
```

```
@Test
public void getChargeForRegular() {
  assertEquals(
    2.0,
    a.movie.w(
      REGULAR).build().getCharge(1),
    0);
  assertEquals(
    2.0,
    a.movie.w(
      REGULAR).build().getCharge(2),
    0);
  assertEquals(
    3.5,
    a.movie.w(
      REGULAR).build().getCharge(3),
    0);
  assertEquals(
    5.0,
    a.movie.w(
      REGULAR).build().getCharge(4),
    0);
}
```

```
@Test
public void getPointsForChildrens() {
  assertEquals(
    1,
    a.movie.w(
      CHILDREN).build().getPoints(1));
  assertEquals(
    1,
    a.movie.w(
      CHILDREN).build().getPoints(2));
}

@Test
public void getPointsForNewRelease() {
  assertEquals(
    1,
    a.movie.w(
      NEW_RELEASE).build().getPoints(1));
  assertEquals(
    2,
    a.movie.w(
      NEW_RELEASE).build().getPoints(2));
  assertEquals(
    2,
    a.movie.w(
      NEW_RELEASE).build().getPoints(3));
}
```

```
@Test
public void getPointsForRegular() {
  assertEquals(
    1,
    a.movie.w(
      REGULAR).build().getPoints(1));
  assertEquals(
    1,
    a.movie.w(
      REGULAR).build().getPoints(2));
}

@Test
(expected=IllegalArgumentException.class)
public void invalidTitle() {
  a.movie.w(UNKNOWN).build();
}
}
```

Movie

```
public class Movie {

  public enum Type {
    REGULAR, NEW_RELEASE, CHILDREN, UNKNOWN;
  }

  private String title;
  Price price;

  public Movie(
    String title, Movie.Type priceCode) {
    this.title = title;
    setPriceCode(priceCode);
  }

  public String getTitle() {
    return title;
  }
```

```
private void setPriceCode(
  Movie.Type priceCode) {
  switch (priceCode) {
  case CHILDREN:
    price = new ChildrensPrice();
    break;
  case NEW_RELEASE:
    price = new NewReleasePrice();
    break;
  case REGULAR:
    price = new RegularPrice();
    break;
  default:
    throw new IllegalArgumentException(
      "invalid price code");
  }
}

public double getCharge(int daysRented) {
  return price.getCharge(daysRented);
}

public int getPoints(int daysRented) {
  return price.getPoints(daysRented);
}
}
```

sociable.RentalTest

```java
public class RentalTest {
  @Test
  public void
  isStartedIfInStoreStateBased() {
    Movie movie = a.movie.build();
    Rental rental =
      a.rental.w(movie).build();
    Store store = a.store.w(movie).build();
    rental.start(store);
    assertTrue(rental.isStarted());
    assertEquals(
      0, store.getAvailability(movie));
  }

  @Test
  public void
  doesNotStartIfNotAvailableStateBased() {
    Movie movie = a.movie.build();
    Rental rental = a.rental.build();
    Store store = a.store.build();
    rental.start(store);
    assertFalse(rental.isStarted());
    assertEquals(
      0, store.getAvailability(movie));
  }
```

```java
@Test
public void
isStartedIfInStoreInteractionBased() {
  Movie movie = a.movie.build();
  Rental rental =
    a.rental.w(movie).build();
  Store store = mock(Store.class);
  when(store.getAvailability(movie))
    .thenReturn(1);
  rental.start(store);
  assertTrue(rental.isStarted());
  verify(store).remove(movie);
}

@Test
public void
notStartedIfUnavailableInteractionBased() {
  Rental rental = a.rental.build();
  Store store = mock(Store.class);
  rental.start(store);
  assertFalse(rental.isStarted());
  verify(
    store, never()).remove(
      any(Movie.class));
}
}
```

Rental

```java
public class Rental {

  Movie movie;
  private int daysRented;
  private boolean started;

  public Rental(
    Movie movie, int daysRented) {
    this.movie = movie;
    this.daysRented = daysRented;
  }

  public Movie getMovie() {
    return movie;
  }

  public int getDaysRented() {
    return daysRented;
  }

  public double getCharge() {
    return movie.getCharge(daysRented);
  }

  public int getPoints() {
    return movie.getPoints(daysRented);
  }
```

```
public String getLineItem() {
  return
    movie.getTitle() + " " + getCharge();
}

public boolean isStarted() {
  return started;
}

public void start(Store store) {
  if (store.getAvailability(movie) > 0) {
    store.remove(movie);
    this.started = true;
  }
}
}
```

Store

```
public class Store {
  private Map<Movie, Integer> movies;

  public Store(Map<Movie, Integer> movies) {
    this.movies = movies;
  }

  public int getAvailability(Movie movie) {
    if (null == movies.get(movie))
      return 0;
    return movies.get(movie);
  }

  public boolean getAvailability(
    Movie movie, int quantity) {
    if (null == movies.get(movie))
      return false;
    return movies.get(movie) >= quantity;
  }

  public void remove(Movie movie) {
    if (null == movies.get(movie))
      return;
    Integer count = movies.get(movie);
    movies.put(movie, --count);
  }
}
```

Improving Assertions

This chapter continues to build on the ideas previously presented, while offering new guidelines with a focus on assertions. The guidelines complement each other, and in many cases following one will put you in a better position to follow others as well.

While some of these ideas may seem unconventional, rest assured that these are pragmatic techniques I've used successfully in various contexts for several years.

While these ideas are not recipes that should be blindly followed in perpetuity, I would recommend trying each of them and deciding which are most effective given your context and motivators.

One Assertion Per Test

Limiting your tests to using one assertion is an especially
controversial topic. I originally stumbled upon the idea on
Dave Astels' blog[12]. I liked the style of development that
Dave described and decided to give it a try, that was over
9 years ago. Since then I've worked on teams ranging from 2-
16 developers, with codebases in Ruby, C#, Clojure, and Java.
Regardless of the context, the guideline has always remained
valuable.

I genuinely believe sticking to one assertion per test will
increase maintainability of your tests. Tests with a tight focus
on one behavior of the system are almost always easier to
write today, and easier to read tomorrow.

Let's look at some code that backs up these promises. The
following example was taken from the previously shown
`MovieTest`. As you can see, this test uses multiple assertions
to verify the charges for a childrens movie.

---

[12]http://www.artima.com/weblogs/viewpost.jsp?thread=35578

```
public class MovieTest {
  @Test
  public void getChargeForChildrens() {
    assertEquals(
      1.5,
      a.movie.w(
        CHILDREN).build().getCharge(1),
      0);
    assertEquals(
      1.5,
      a.movie.w(
        CHILDREN).build().getCharge(2),
      0);
    assertEquals(
      1.5,
      a.movie.w(
        CHILDREN).build().getCharge(3),
      0);
    assertEquals(
      3.0,
      a.movie.w(
        CHILDREN).build().getCharge(4),
      0);
    assertEquals(
      4.5,
      a.movie.w(
        CHILDREN).build().getCharge(5),
      0);
  }
}
```

Failure

The above test is passing, but a small change to `ChildrensPrice` will generate a failure. Below you'll find the JUnit output when the test above is failing.

```
JUnit version 4.11
.E
There was 1 failure:
1) getChargeForChildrens(solitary.MovieTest)
java.lang.AssertionError: expected:<1.5> but was:\
<3.0>

FAILURES!!!
Tests run: 1,  Failures: 1
```

The example above demonstrates the first reason I dislike multiple asserts in one test. The first failure occurred when calling `getCharge` with 3. We're able to find that data by looking at the (unincluded) stacktrace. It's a bit annoying to have to look at the stacktrace to know what's failing, but that alone wouldn't drive me to break this test into multiple tests. My largest complaint with this test is that I now know of one failure, but have no (automatically generated) information about the remaining tests.

Given a test with multiple assertions, when they're all passing they all provide value; however, when an assertion fails it removes any value that would have been provided by all subsequent assertions.

Below you can find the simple change that caused the tests to begin failing.

```
public class ChildrensPrice extends Price {

  @Override
  public double getCharge(int daysRented) {
    double amount = 1.5;
    if (daysRented > 2) // *was 3*
      amount += (daysRented - 2) * 1.5;
    return amount;
  }
}
```

> At this point you may wonder if the collaboration between Movie and ChildrensPrice forces MovieTest to be classified as a *Sociable Unit Test.* That's definitely an interesting question, and one that we'll explore later in the book.

When faced with a failing test with multiple assertions you're forced to select from two inferior choices while (unnecessarily) working with limited information. You must either read the domain code and test code to determine if any of the additional assertions would fail, or you'll have to loop between running the tests and fixing any new failures. Both approaches are inferior to running the tests once and being presented with all of the pass/fail information.

Test Naming

I've already confessed that I don't find much value in test names. However, I also pointed out that they're required by most frameworks, and I think it's in everyone's best interest if we spend the time to create helpful names. The currently failing test has the name `getChargeForChildrens`, which points me at a `Movie.getCharge` and provides the value of one of the parameters, but it doesn't tell me anything about the only argument that's actually passed to `getCharge`. I can't see any reason why the `MovieType` (CHILDREN) is more important than the number of days the movie was rented. We could have written the `MovieTest` methods grouped by `daysRented` instead, though the names would be just as limited and the groupings just as unhelpful.

The Solution

You already know how these tests are going to look, but I'd like to look at something else before I confirm your suspicions. Below you'll find the results of testing the same domain code using one assertion per test.

```
JUnit version 4.11
...E.E.E
There were 3 failures:
1) getChargeForChildrens3Day(solitary.MovieTest)
java.lang.AssertionError: expected:<1.5> but was:\
<3.0>
2) getChargeForChildrens4Day(solitary.MovieTest)
java.lang.AssertionError: expected:<3.0> but was:\
<4.5>
3) getChargeForChildrens5Day(solitary.MovieTest)
java.lang.AssertionError: expected:<4.5> but was:\
<6.0>

FAILURES!!!
Tests run: 5,   Failures: 3
```

It's hard to express how much I prefer these failures to the last presented failure. The test names give me a good description of what's failing. The expected and return values give me valuable information per test, and the sum of the expected and return values gives me additional information. Specifically, It's very easy to spot the pattern: *anything above 2 days is failing, and each failure is off by 1.5.* Anytime you put multiple asserts in a test you're suppressing valuable pattern information that could help you (or more importantly a teammate) find the source of a failure.

Below you'll find the updated MovieTest with one assertion per test.

```
public class MovieTest {
  @Test
  public void getChargeForChildrens1Day() {
    assertEquals(
      1.5,
      a.movie.w(
        CHILDREN).build().getCharge(1),
      0);
  }

  @Test
  public void getChargeForChildrens2Day() {
    assertEquals(
      1.5,
      a.movie.w(
        CHILDREN).build().getCharge(2),
      0);
  }

  @Test
  public void getChargeForChildrens3Day() {
    assertEquals(
      1.5,
      a.movie.w(
        CHILDREN).build().getCharge(3),
      0);
  }
```

```
@Test
public void getChargeForChildrens4Day() {
  assertEquals(
    3.0,
    a.movie.w(
      CHILDREN).build().getCharge(4),
    0);
}

@Test
public void getChargeForChildrens5Day() {
  assertEquals(
    4.5,
    a.movie.w(
      CHILDREN).build().getCharge(5),
    0);
  }
}
```

Applying One Assertion Per Test To Behavior Verification Tests

The previous example focused exclusively on *State Verification* tests; however, I believe it's important to apply the guideline to *Behavior Verification* tests as well. To be completely clear: verifying a mock is asserting something, and I strongly suggest you have one and only one assertion per test.

As usual we'll start with an example. The following test is the first interaction test we introduced in Chapter 3, refactored to use a mock for the movie (thus making it a *Solitary Unit Test*).

```
public class RentalTest {
  @Test
  public void rentalIsStartedIfInStore() {
    Movie movie = mock(Movie.class);
    Rental rental =
      a.rental.w(movie).build();
    Store store = mock(Store.class);
    when(store.getAvailability(movie))
      .thenReturn(1);
    rental.start(store);
    assertTrue(rental.isStarted());
    verify(store).remove(movie);
  }
}
```

My concerns with this test are very similar to my concerns in the previous test: the test name doesn't convey any intent for Store, and the first assertion to fail strips all additional value from the assertions that follow the failure.

The test name could be altered to include Store, e.g. rentalIsStartedAndMovieIsRemovedFromStoreIfMovieCurrentlyInStore

Some would argue the long test name is fine; in my experience the longer the name the faster it tends to degrade. Additionally, many believe the word "*and*" in a test name is an indicator that your test needs to be split into at least 2 smaller tests. While I can't claim to have invented the advice, I definitely agree with it.

The following failure output and test demonstrate the second issue.

```
JUnit version 4.11
.E
There was 1 failure:
1) rentalIsStartedIfInStore(solitary.RentalTest)
java.lang.AssertionError

FAILURES!!!
Tests run: 1,  Failures: 1
```

```
public class RentalTest {
  @Test
  public void rentalIsStartedIfInStore() {
    Movie movie = mock(Movie.class);
    Rental rental =
      a.rental.w(movie).build();
    Store store = mock(Store.class);
    when(store.getAvailability(movie, 1))
      .thenReturn(true);
    rental.start(store);
    assertTrue(rental.isStarted());
    verify(store).remove(movie);
  }
}
```

In the above example I switched the stubbing of the store
getAvailability(Movie) to getAvailability(Movie, int).
A common real-life scenario is a switch of the domain code
from one method to another, and a stubbing that's now out
of date. The result would look exactly like the failure above.
Unfortunately, the failure provides no answer to the question
Was remove called on the Store mock?

The solution is straightforward, test the Rental state in RentalTest
and test the Store behavior in the StoreTest.

After moving the Store verification to StoreTest there are
several small improvements we can make to the
rentalIsStartedIfInStore test.

```
public class RentalTest {
  @Test
  public void rentalIsStartedIfInStore() {
    Rental rental = a.rental.build();
    Store store = mock(Store.class);
    when(store
        .getAvailability(any(Movie.class)))
      .thenReturn(1);
    rental.start(store);
    assertTrue(rental.isStarted());
  }
}
```

The example above is the simplified RentalTest. The latest version makes no attempt to verify interactions with the store mock, thus removing the need to create a local Movie variable. The RentalBuilder creates its own Movie (stub), and the store.getAvailability method stubbing can be switched to return 1 for any instance of Movie. The resulting test is easier to read (less code to digest), and also more robust (generalization of stub arguments make this test more resilient to changes in the collaborator).

With the RentalTest improved, we can turn our attention to creating a StoreTest. The Store domain object contains fairly simple state; state that has no explicit dependency on Rental. The following tests demonstrate how the Store class can be easily verified using a *Solitary Unit Test.*

```java
public class StoreTest {
  @Test
  public void storeWithNoAvailability() {
    Store store = a.store.build();
    assertEquals(
      0,
      store.getAvailability(
        mock(Movie.class)));
  }

  @Test
  public void storeWithAvailability() {
    Movie movie = mock(Movie.class);
    Store store =
      a.store.w(movie, movie).build();
    assertEquals(
      2, store.getAvailability(movie));
  }

  @Test
  public void
  storeWithRemovedAvailability() {
    Movie movie = mock(Movie.class);
    Store store =
      a.store.w(movie, movie).build();
    store.remove(movie);
    assertEquals(
      1, store.getAvailability(movie));
  }
}
```

The three simple *State Verification* tests above are so straight-forward I can't see much about them worth mentioning.

Those are the types of tests that I prefer to maintain - self explanatory tests.

The RentalTest and StoreTest *Solitary Unit Tests* would give me plenty of confidence in the system; however, this also feels like a great place for a *Sociable Unit Test.*

```java
public class RentalTest {
  @Test
  public void
  storeAvailabilityIsModifiedOnRental() {
    Movie movie = a.movie.build();
    Rental rental =
      a.rental.w(movie).build();
    Store store =
      a.store.w(movie, movie).build();
    rental.start(store);
    a.rental.build().start(store);
    assertEquals(
      1, store.getAvailability(movie));
  }
}
```

The *Sociable Unit Test* above verifies that starting a Rental will correctly remove a movie from inventory.

Thoughts On The Result

Tests with one assertion or mock verification clearly express their purpose. In general, I believe code should not only express how it works, but also why it's been written in a particular way. The new tests not only execute, but convey their intent as well. Our new tests take more lines of code than the original, but are also more maintainable. You could change the internal implementation of Store in various ways without impacting the RentalTest *Solitary Unit Tests*. When the implementation does inevitably change these tests communicate the original author's intent.

Writing tests in this way is easy, but does require discipline.

- If your test has an assertion, do not add any mock verifications.
- If your test verifies a mock, do not add any assertions.
- At most, 1 assertion per test.
- At most, 1 mock verification per test.
- When stubbing method return values, use the most generic argument matcher possible. Which segues nicely to...

Implementation Overspecification

The following Customer class contains a new method: recentRentals

```
public class Customer {

  private String name;
  private List<Rental> rentals =
    new ArrayList<Rental>();

  public Customer(String name) {
    this.name = name;
  }

  public void addRental(Rental rental) {
    rentals.add(rental);
  }

  public String recentRentals() {
    String result = "Recent rentals:";
    for (int i=0;
         i < rentals.size() && i < 3;
         i++) {
      result += "\n" +
        rentals.get(i).getMovie(
          true).getTitle(
            "%s starring %s %s", 2);
    }
    return result;
  }
}
```

The recentRentals method returns a string that contains the
titles of up to 3 *recent rentals* - thus it makes sense to create
tests for Customer instances with 2, 3, and 4 rentals.

You may have also noticed that both `Movie.getTitle` and `Rental.getMovie` now require arguments. The arguments being passed to `getTitle` are a format string and the number of actors to include - and that's all you really need to know about `getTitle`. Calling `getTitle` will be important for this section, but the actual implementation is irrelevant. Similarly, the `boolean` passed to `getMovie` indicates whether the `Movie` returned will be a copy or the original `Rental` constructor argument, but the implementation isn't relevant for the following examples.

Below you'll find multiple tests for the `recentRentals` method. If you've ever used a mocking framework, it's likely that you've written unit tests that look like the following examples.

```java
public class CustomerTest {
  @Test
  public void recentRentalsWith2Rentals() {
    Movie godfather = mock(Movie.class);
    when(godfather
        .getTitle("%s starring %s %s", 2))
      .thenReturn("Godfather 4");
    Rental godfatherRental =
      mock(Rental.class);
    when(godfatherRental.getMovie(true))
      .thenReturn(godfather);
    Movie lionKing = mock(Movie.class);
    when(lionKing
        .getTitle("%s starring %s %s", 2))
      .thenReturn("Lion King");
    Rental lionKingRental =
      mock(Rental.class);
    when(lionKingRental.getMovie(true))
      .thenReturn(lionKing);

    assertEquals(
      "Recent rentals:\nGodfather 4\n" +
      "Lion King",
      a.customer.w(
        godfatherRental, lionKingRental)
      .build().recentRentals());
}
```

```
@Test
public void recentRentalsWith3Rentals() {
  // same structure as above, with
  // 8 more lines of mocking code,
  // 25% longer expected value, and
  // 2 lines of adding rentals to customer
}

@Test
public void recentRentalsWith4Rentals() {
  // same structure as above, with
  // 16 more lines of mocking code,
  // 25% longer expected value, and
  // 2 lines of adding rentals to customer
}
}
```

The point of this section would really be emphasized by writing out all 3 tests, but I couldn't bring myself to do that to people reading on mobile devices. Hopefully it's not too hard to imagine how brutal and unnecessary it would be to see the above example repeated and increased by 50 to 100 percent.

These tests are painful to read, but the greater issue is how brittle they become as the business logic changes. Few things kill productivity and motivation more than cascading test failures, and implementation overspecification is a common cause of cascading failures.

- A change to the Movie.getTitle definition could cause this test to fail, e.g. this test would fail if a Title class were introduced and became the return value of getTitle.

- Any change to the `Rental.getMovie` definition could cause this test to fail similarly to the above example.
- Any change to the arguments passed to `getTitle` or `getMovie` would cascade through the above and the 2 (unwritten) tests.
- As implementations change it's not uncommon for method calls to become superfluous, causing any stubbing of the unused methods to become superfluous as well. Since stubbing a method causes no failure it's very common to find stubbing that is no longer relevant to an otherwise valuable test.

It's very common to add arguments, rename, overload, and replace methods. The more specification your tests contain the more likely you are to create a brittle test suite.

Flexible Argument Matchers

The first simple change you can make to reduce cascading failures is to introduce a flexible argument matcher. The method we're interested in testing returns a `String`. It shouldn't matter to the test what `String`, `int`, & `boolean` arguments are used to accomplish this task.

The following unit tests make use of *Mockito's* `anyString`, `anyInt`, and `anyBoolean` matchers.

```java
public class CustomerTest {
  @Test
  public void recentRentalsWith2Rentals() {
    Movie godfather = mock(Movie.class);
    when(
      godfather.getTitle(
        anyString(), anyInt()))
      .thenReturn("Godfather 4");
    Rental godfatherRental =
      mock(Rental.class);
    when(
      godfatherRental.getMovie(anyBoolean()))
      .thenReturn(godfather);
    Movie lionKing = mock(Movie.class);
    when(
      lionKing.getTitle(
        anyString(), anyInt()))
      .thenReturn("Lion King");
    Rental lionKingRental =
      mock(Rental.class);
    when(
      lionKingRental.getMovie(anyBoolean()))
      .thenReturn(lionKing);

    assertEquals(
      "Recent rentals:\nGodfather 4\n" +
      "Lion King",
      a.customer.w(
        godfatherRental, lionKingRental)
      .build().recentRentals());
  }
}
```

This simple change completely removes any cascading failures that would occur from changing any of the argument values passed to getTitle and getMovie. The resulting tests are free to focus less on the implementation and more on the assertion's expected value.

Default Return Values

We're specifying return values for both the getMovie and getTitle methods. The return value for getMovie is necessary to avoid a NullPointerException; however, do we really need a return value for getTitle?

```
public class CustomerTest {
  @Test
  public void recentRentalsWith2Rentals() {
    Movie godfather = mock(Movie.class);
    Rental godfatherRental =
      mock(Rental.class);
    when(
      godfatherRental.getMovie(anyBoolean()))
      .thenReturn(godfather);
    Movie lionKing = mock(Movie.class);
    Rental lionKingRental =
      mock(Rental.class);
    when(
      lionKingRental.getMovie(anyBoolean()))
      .thenReturn(lionKing);

    assertEquals(
      "Recent rentals:\nnull\nnull",
      a.customer.w(
        godfatherRental, lionKingRental)
      .build().recentRentals());
  }
}
```

The above test removes the return value specification for getTitle. A nice side-effect of removing the return value is the ability to remove the method stubbing completely; flexible matchers are great, but specifying nothing will always be superior. Increasing test durability and removing code (thus conceptual overhead) are always preferable, but at what cost? I would argue that testing for the String "null" is no better or worse than testing for the String "Godfather 4". However, I'm happy to concede that without specifying the return values we have lost any assertion on ordering. We'll come back to that.

You may have noticed that our assertion now makes no differentiation between the two rentals; thus there's really no need for two Movie and Rental instances.

```java
public class CustomerTest {
  @Test
  public void recentRentalsWith2Rentals() {
    Movie movie = mock(Movie.class);
    Rental rental = mock(Rental.class);
    when(rental.getMovie(anyBoolean()))
      .thenReturn(movie);
    assertEquals(
      "Recent rentals:\nnull\nnull",
      a.customer.w(rental, rental).build()
      .recentRentals());
  }
}
```

Law of Demeter

At this point we've simplified our tests to the level that adding the previously unwritten tests would be as easy as copying what we have and adding rental as many times as necessary. However, before we pursue that path it's worth mentioning another possible improvement.

As I previously mentioned in Behavior Verification, people who tend to use mocks also tend not to violate the Law of Demeter.

Law of Demeter[13] can be succinctly summarized in one of the

---

[13]http://en.wikipedia.org/wiki/Law_of_Demeter

following ways:

- Each unit should have only limited knowledge about other units: only units "closely" related to the current unit.
- Each unit should only talk to its friends; don't talk to strangers.
- Only talk to your immediate friends.

As I previously mentioned, the #isTDDDead debate has been a hot topic lately. In response, Gary Bernhardt wrote[14] the following.

> [E]xperienced users of mocks rarely nest them deeply. Avoiding numerous or deeply nested mocks is the principal design activity of isolated TDD.

I believe Gary's opinion is absolutely correct. I would actually argue that the advice has little to do with TDD and should be more broadly applied. I would restate it as the following:

> Experienced users of mocks rarely nest them deeply. Avoiding numerous or deeply nested mocks is a principal design activity for people who effectively use mocks.

Indeed, the impact of applying the Law of Demeter can be seen by looking at the resulting test.

---

[14]https://www.destroyallsoftware.com/blog/2014/test-isolation-is-about-avoiding-mocks

```java
public class CustomerTest {
  @Test
  public void recentRentalsWith2Rentals() {
    Rental rental = mock(Rental.class);
    assertEquals(
      "Recent rentals:\nnull\nnull",
      a.customer.w(rental, rental).build()
      .recentRentals());
  }
}
```

A change must obviously be made to Rental to enable the test above. Below you can find the updated Customer domain class, which relies on the getTitle method of Rental.

> note: In our Customer implementation we pass no arguments to getTitle. Whether or not getTitle can use defaults or should take arguments will depend on your domain and is outside the scope of our discussion; our test would look the same regardless of the arguments taken by getTitle.

```java
public class Customer {

  private String name;
  private List<Rental> rentals =
    new ArrayList<Rental>();

  public Customer(String name) {
    this.name = name;
  }

  public void addRental(Rental rental) {
    rentals.add(rental);
  }

  public String recentRentals() {
    String result = "Recent rentals:";
    for (int i=0;
         i < rentals.size() && i < 3;
         i++) {
      result +=
        "\n" + rentals.get(i).getTitle();
    }
    return result;
  }
}
```

Martin Fowler points out (in *Mocks aren't Stubs*) this type of change can lead to *middle men objects bloated with forwarding methods*. Whether or not to make this final change will often rest with the test maintainer and their opinion on the impact to the domain model. I would tend to err on the side of following the Law of Demeter, as it allows me to enjoy the benefits of many tests while ensuring that they are succinct

enough to maintain. For example, I would prefer to test the
recentRentals method using customers with 0, 1, 2, 3, and 4
rentals. Below, you can find exactly those tests.

```java
public class CustomerTest {
  @Test
  public void recentRentals0Rentals() {
    assertEquals(
      "Recent rentals:",
      a.customer.build().recentRentals());
  }

  @Test
  public void recentRentals1Rental() {
    assertEquals(
      "Recent rentals:\nnull",
      a.customer.w(
        mock(Rental.class)).build()
      .recentRentals());
  }

  @Test
  public void recentRentals2Rental() {
    assertEquals(
      "Recent rentals:\nnull\nnull",
      a.customer.w(
        mock(Rental.class),
        mock(Rental.class)).build()
      .recentRentals());
  }
```

```
@Test
public void recentRentals3Rental() {
  assertEquals(
    "Recent rentals:\nnull\nnull\nnull",
    a.customer.w(
      mock(Rental.class),
      mock(Rental.class),
      mock(Rental.class)).build()
    .recentRentals());
}

@Test
public void recentRentals4Rental() {
  assertEquals(
    "Recent rentals:\nnull\nnull\nnull",
    a.customer.w(
      mock(Rental.class),
      mock(Rental.class),
      mock(Rental.class),
      mock(Rental.class)).build()
    .recentRentals());
}
}
```

I believe it's worth noting that increasing the quality of the tests put me in a position to easily increase test coverage as well.

Get Sociable

Our *Solitary Unit Tests* succinctly cover most of the functionality of recentRentals. If you find yourself concerned about changes to Rental or Movie not being detected by our current tests, I would point out that this is by design. I wouldn't want changes in either of those classes to affect Customer tests unless it were unavoidable. Tests ensuring changes to Rental or Movie do not produce production bugs should live in RentalTest and MovieTest respectively.

While the *Solitary Unit Tests* do provide valuable coverage, we still need to test that the actual domain classes compose correctly and in the expected order (the coverage I previously noted the loss of).

Below you can find a *Sociable Unit Test* that covers those concerns.

```
public class CustomerTest {
  @Test
  public void
  recentRentalsWith3OrderedRentals() {
    assertEquals(
      "Recent rentals:"+
      "\nGodfather 4\nLion King\nScarface",
      a.customer.w(
        a.rental.w(a.movie.w("Godfather 4")),
        a.rental.w(a.movie.w("Lion King")),
        a.rental.w(a.movie.w("Scarface")),
        a.rental.w(a.movie.w("Notebook")))
      .build().recentRentals());
  }
}
```

By combining a single *Sociable Unit Test* with several *Solitary Unit Tests* utilizing sparsely specified mocks we're able to cover all functionality while avoiding cascading failures, accidental coupling, and overly verbose tests.

Comparison

I couldn't bring myself to end this chapter without providing a few examples for comparison. I think it's worth noting that all of the *Solitary Unit Tests* combined are less lines of code than the original individual test with 4 rentals.

The (Previously Unwritten) Original Test with Four Rentals

```java
public class CustomerTest {
  @Test
  public void recentRentalsWith4Rentals() {
    Movie godfather = mock(Movie.class);
    when(godfather
        .getTitle("%s starring %s %s", 2))
      .thenReturn("Godfather 4");
    Rental godfatherRental =
      mock(Rental.class);
    when(godfatherRental.getMovie(true))
      .thenReturn(godfather);
    Movie lionKing = mock(Movie.class);
    when(lionKing
        .getTitle("%s starring %s %s", 2))
      .thenReturn("Lion King");
    Rental lionKingRental =
      mock(Rental.class);
    when(lionKingRental.getMovie(true))
      .thenReturn(lionKing);
    Movie scarface = mock(Movie.class);
    when(scarface
        .getTitle("%s starring %s %s", 2))
      .thenReturn("Scarface");
    Rental scarfaceRental =
      mock(Rental.class);
    when(scarfaceRental.getMovie(true))
      .thenReturn(scarface);
    Movie notebook = mock(Movie.class);
    when(notebook
        .getTitle("%s starring %s %s", 2))
```

```
      .thenReturn("Notebook");
    Rental notebookRental =
      mock(Rental.class);
    when(notebookRental.getMovie(true))
      .thenReturn(notebook);

    assertEquals(
      "Recent rentals:"+
      "\nGodfather 4\nLion King" +
      "\nScarface",
      a.customer.w(
        godfatherRental, lionKingRental,
        scarfaceRental, notebookRental)
      .build().recentRentals());
  }
}
```

The Sociable Unit Test and The Sparsely Specified Solitary Unit Tests

Sociable CustomerTest

```java
public class CustomerTest {
  @Test
  public void
  recentRentalsWith3OrderedRentals() {
    assertEquals(
      "Recent rentals:"+
      "\nGodfather 4\nLion King\nScarface",
      a.customer.w(
        a.rental.w(a.movie.w("Godfather 4")),
        a.rental.w(a.movie.w("Lion King")),
        a.rental.w(a.movie.w("Scarface")),
        a.rental.w(a.movie.w("Notebook")))
      .build().recentRentals());
  }
}
```

Solitary CustomerTest

```java
public class CustomerTest {
  @Test
  public void recentRentals0Rentals() {
    assertEquals(
      "Recent rentals:",
      a.customer.build().recentRentals());
  }

  @Test
  public void recentRentals1Rental() {
    assertEquals(
      "Recent rentals:\nnull",
      a.customer.w(
        mock(Rental.class)).build()
      .recentRentals());
  }

  @Test
  public void recentRentals2Rental() {
    assertEquals(
      "Recent rentals:\nnull\nnull",
      a.customer.w(
        mock(Rental.class),
        mock(Rental.class)).build()
      .recentRentals());
  }
```

```
@Test
public void recentRentals3Rental() {
  assertEquals(
    "Recent rentals:\nnull\nnull\nnull",
    a.customer.w(
      mock(Rental.class),
      mock(Rental.class),
      mock(Rental.class)).build()
    .recentRentals());
}

@Test
public void recentRentals4Rental() {
  assertEquals(
    "Recent rentals:\nnull\nnull\nnull",
    a.customer.w(
      mock(Rental.class),
      mock(Rental.class),
      mock(Rental.class),
      mock(Rental.class)).build()
    .recentRentals());
}
}
```

There's vast power in creating a domain model that can be succinctly tested.

Assert Last

The longer a test takes to digest, the more likely I am to be unhappy with it. This process usually begins by trying to find the actual 'assertion'. Rather than starting with examples of tests I find inferior, I'll begin by defining what I call the Assert Last principle: The assertion should be the last piece of code found within a test.

You may have run into a similar idea in the past. There are a few *AAA* definitions that can be found on the web:

> *Assemble Activate Assert* seems to be used primarily in the Ruby Language community. The *Arrange Act Assert* term seems to be more popular in the Java Language community.

> "Arrange-Act-Assert" is a pattern for arranging and formatting code in Unit Test methods. Each method should group the following, separated by blank lines: *Arrange all necessary preconditions and inputs. Act on the object or method under test. Assert that the expected results have occurred.* c2 wiki[15]

Assert Last is a subset of *AAA*, and it's the *A* that I've found to have the most value. Your tests will become more maintainable if you can convince your team to go full *AAA*. However, if you're not ready to go full *AAA*, I believe you can still get 80% of the benefit simply by adopting the *Assert Last* guideline.

---

[15]http://c2.com/cgi/wiki?AssembleActivateAssert

Many of the problematic tests you've seen up to this point violate this principle.

- Tests with multiple assertions often end with an assertion, but also contain interleaved assertions as well. As we previously noted, multiple assertions force the maintainer to determine which assertion actually failed. Boo.
- Tests with assertions in loops somewhat structurally appear to end with a single assertion, but we've already seen how incorrect it would be to claim those tests follow the principle.
- Testing an expected exception via an Annotation clearly violates this principle.

We've already seen two of the three solutions: One Assertion Per Test & Replace Loop with Individual Test respectively.

Unfortunately testing exceptions while following this principle is a bit less friendly on the eyes.

Expect Exceptions via Try/Catch

The starting point for this section will be the invalidTitle test that was last seen in the Final Thoughts section of Chapter 3.

```
public class MovieTest {
  @Test
  (expected=IllegalArgumentException.class)
  public void invalidTitle() {
    a.movie.w(UNKNOWN).build();
  }
}
```

In Chapter 3 I called this test a *"good"* test; however, perhaps I was a bit too generous. That test is a good example of a *Solitary Unit Test*; however, it's not what I would consider a *good* test. Despite being very simple, I still dislike this test based solely on its violation of the Assert Last principle. It feels unnecessary to say this, and yet I can't bring myself to be less than explicit: there's a cost to breaking patterns, and putting your assertion in an Annotation simply to avoid the characters necessary to write a try / catch is very short-sighted.

```java
public class MovieTest {
  @Test
  public void invalidTitle() {
    try {
      a.movie.w(UNKNOWN).build();
      fail();
    } catch (Exception ex) {
      assertEquals(
        IllegalArgumentException.class,
        ex.getClass());
    }
  }
}
```

The above test is usually what you find when someone doesn't know about or disapproves of the expected exception Annotation. While it does the trick, it also violates the Assert Last principle. When the first line of the try block fails to throw an exception, Assert.fail is invoked. I consider fail to be an assertion not found last within the test. However, even if I didn't consider fail an assertion, this test structure has another large problem: If the fail is forgotten at the time of test creation the test will pass, but at some point (if the exception stops being thrown) the test will begin reporting false positives due to the catch no longer being executed.

The following test is even more verbose, but provides no opportunities for false positives.

```
public class MovieTest {
  @Test
  public void invalidTitle() {
    Exception e = null;
    try {
      a.movie.w(UNKNOWN).build();
    } catch (Exception ex) {
      e = ex;
    }
    assertEquals(
      IllegalArgumentException.class,
      e.getClass());
  }
}
```

Assert Throws

Although the above test structure suffices it isn't exactly
elegant. Perhaps it's worth taking a step back. We've all been
told that exceptions shouldn't be used for flow control, and
I'm violating that advice in this example. Sometimes it is
worth taking a step back to ask if an ugly test is giving an
indication of a poor domain choices. Is it possible to change
the domain code to make it follow best practices (no flow
control exceptions) and be more testable?

Still, I'm sure there are codebases where a large number of
exceptions are raised for valid reasons. In that case, I suspect
you may want to create some infrastructure to remove the
test noise. Below you'll find an example of a test that uses a
user defined assertThrows method

```
public class MovieTest {
  @Test
  public void invalidTitle() {
    Runnable runnable = new Runnable() {
        public void run() {
          a.movie.w(UNKNOWN).build();
        }
      };
    assertThrows(
      IllegalArgumentException.class,
      runnable);
  }

  public void assertThrows(
    Class ex, Runnable runnable) {
    Exception exThrown = null;
    try {
      runnable.run();
    } catch (Exception exThrownActual) {
      exThrown = exThrownActual;
    }
    if (null == exThrown)
      fail("No exception thrown");
    else
      assertEquals(ex, exThrown.getClass());
  }
}
```

I'm not crazy enough to call the above solution 'elegant' in its current form. However, if you're already using IntelliJ the anonymous Runnable class will collapse to something much more palatable. Additionally, Java 8's lambda syntax could be used to create a pleasant, yet concise solution (and will be, later).

Mock Verification

Thus far, all *Behavior Verification* examples found in this book have used the Mockito mock framework. Mockito's mocks allow interaction without specification; verification of mocks is always done following the interaction via the verify method. Mockito's interaction style allows for seamless conformance to the Assert Last principle. The same cannot be said of many competing frameworks.

Many of the competing frameworks have loyal users and advocates. I strongly believe that people should use the tools that make them the most effective, thus I would never go so far as to recommend everyone switch to Mockito and my style of testing. That said, if you've never attempted to write your tests with the Assert Last principle in mind, I believe you should give it a try at some point. There's something truly satisfying and productive about working with tests where you know, before even looking at the test, that whatever is being verified can be found at the end of the test.

Comparison

I like to end these sections with examples that are easy to compare. My hope is that these comparison subsections give you the opportunity to decide if the advice applies to you or not.

> note: a setPrice method was added to Movie strictly to enable a *Behavior Verification* test example. Were this more than a book example, I would likely use a *State Verification* test to verify getCharge (as has been previously shown) and I would have no need for the setPrice method.

Inconsistent Assert Location

```java
public class MovieTest {
  Mockery context = new Mockery();

  @Test
  public void getPointsForDays() {
    Movie movie = a.movie.build();
    assertEquals(1, movie.getPoints(2));
    assertEquals(1, movie.getPoints(3));
  }

  @Test
  (expected=IllegalArgumentException.class)
  public void invalidTitle() {
    a.movie.w(UNKNOWN).build();
  }

  @Test
  public void getPriceFromPriceInstance() {
    final Price price =
      context.mock(Price.class);
    Movie movie = a.movie.build();
    movie.setPrice(price);

    context.checking(new Expectations() {{
      oneOf(price).getCharge(3);
    }});

    movie.getCharge(3);
    context.assertIsSatisfied();
  }
}
```

Although the word 'assert' is used on the last line of the JMock test, the actual expectations are found much higher in the test.

Assert Last Conformance

```
public class MovieTest {
  @Test
  public void getPoints2Days() {
    assertEquals(
      2, a.movie.build().getPoints(2));
  }

  @Test
  public void getPoints3Days() {
    assertEquals(
      2, a.movie.build().getPoints(3));
  }

  @Test
  public void invalidTitle() {
    Runnable runnable = new Runnable() {
        public void run() {
          a.movie.w(UNKNOWN).build();
        }
      };
    assertThrows(
      IllegalArgumentException.class,
      runnable);
  }
```

```
@Test
public void getPriceFromPriceInstance() {
  Price price = mock(Price.class);
  Movie movie = a.movie.build();
  movie.setPrice(price);
  movie.getCharge(3);
  verify(price).getCharge(3);
 }
}
```

I find the Assert Last principle to have a sum value that's greater than the parts (i.e. the value is in consistent application of the principle across an entire codebase, not in an individual test).

Expect Literals

When writing a *State Verification* test you must specify an expected and actual value. Though there are several static methods on `Assert` that can be used for verification, `assertEquals` is by far the most commonly used assertion. When using `assertEquals` your *State Verification* test takes the shape `assertEquals(expected, actual)`.

Expected values can be any object; however, using literals (`String`, `int`, `char`) for expected values is advantageous for readability and traceability. To be clear, the expected value should be the literal itself, not a variable holding a value that was previously created by a literal.

Tests that use literal *expected* values are easier to read; when an expected value is simply a literal you're able to focus almost exclusively on the *actual* value. The following 3 tests verify the same thing, but only the third example uses a literal expected value. In the third example it's easy to see what's expected, less so in the first two.

> note: the following example asserts equality on doubles, thus the generic format is `assertEquals(expected, actual, delta)`

```java
public class RegularPriceTest {
  @Test
  public void chargeWithStaticVal() {
    assertEquals(
      basePrice,
      a.regularPrice.build().getCharge(2),
      0);
  }

  @Test
  public void chargeWithLocalVal() {
    int daysRented = 4;
    double charge =
      basePrice + (
        daysRented - 2) * multiplier;
    assertEquals(
      charge,
      a.regularPrice.build().getCharge(
        daysRented),
      0);
  }

  @Test
  public void chargeWithLiteral() {
    assertEquals(
      5.0,
      a.regularPrice.build().getCharge(4),
      0);
  }
}
```

The above tests are fairly clean by design. Even with simplified tests the second example shows how things can escalate

quickly when an expected value is more than a literal. The value of expecting literals becomes even greater as the tests become more complex. As we noted in Chapter 1, if neither your expected nor actual values are literals you're forced to determine the value of both when a test fails. Conversely, if your expected value is a literal, only the *actual* value will need to be traced when a test is failing.

In the above example, if the final test fails it's due to the calculation changing in some way - there's no other possible cause. When the calculation changes, it's valuable to get feedback that it changed (by way of a failing test). The second test doesn't use a literal expected value, and it will not fail if the value of `multiplier` is changed. Some people might consider this valuable or perhaps even more maintainable, I'd consider it a bug waiting to happen.

Despite who's writing the code, it's not likely that the programmer is actually responsible for determining the correct multiplier based on business needs. Most businesses would have a subject matter expert that would provide the multiplier and express (via requirements) the formula for calculating a charge.

It seems safe to assume the requirements will give examples such as:

- a 2 day rental = charge of 2.0
- a 3 day rental = charge of 3.5
- a 4 day rental = charge of 5.0

If literal numbers are used as expected values the tests will directly reflect some or all of the examples from the business, giving us confidence that the calculation has been written as the business desires. In the future, when the requirements change, new literals can be added to the tests before the calculation is updated.

Given this work-flow, it shouldn't be possible to accidentally break the calculation; by decoupling the expected value from the domain, we've increased the value of our tests.

Value Objects vs Expect Literals

There are times when the language doesn't provide a literal for the actual value. For example, when you need to assert equality on a value object such as a Money, Date or Time. In that situation I do my best to use literal expected values and convert the value object to a literal that approximates the value as closely as possible. In the case of a Money object I would likely do something along the lines of assertEquals(10.0, tenDollars.toDouble(), 0). The following example demonstrates the solution I would choose for dealing with a Movie.releaseDate.

```
public class MovieTest {
  @Test
  public void compareDates() {
    Movie godfather =
      a.movie.w(
        new Date(70261200000L)).build();
    assertEquals(
      "1972-03-24",
      new SimpleDateFormat(
        "yyyy-MM-dd").format(
          godfather.releaseDate())));
  }
}
```

It's not always possible to use literals for expected values, but if you strive to use literals whenever possible your tests will be more readable and traceable.

Comparison

As I previously mentioned, the tests within this section were kept quite simple by design. Hopefully the concise (yet contrived) tests effectively convey the point. If so, you can skim or skip the next examples; however, if you find yourself unconvinced, here's a quick comparison using examples from Chapter 1.

Expecting Variables

```
public class CustomerTest {
  @Test
  public void statementFor1Rental() {
    Rental rental = mock(Rental.class);
    Customer customer =
      a.customer.w(rental).build();

    assertEquals(
      expStatement(
        "Rental record for %s\n%sAmount " +
        "owed is %s\n" +
        "You earned %s frequent " +
        "renter points",
        customer,
        rentalInfo(
          "\t", "", new Rental[] {rental})),
      customer.statement());
  }
```

```java
@Test
public void statementFor2Rentals() {
  Rental godfather = mock(Rental.class);
  Rental scarface = mock(Rental.class);
  Customer customer =
    a.customer.w(
      godfather, scarface).build();

  assertEquals(
    expStatement(
      "Rental record for %s\n%sAmount " +
      "owed is %s\n" +
      "You earned %s frequent " +
      "renter points",
      customer,
      rentalInfo(
        "\t", "", new Rental[] {
          godfather, scarface})),
    customer.statement());
}
```

```
public static String rentalInfo(
  String startsWith,
  String endsWith,
  Rental[] rentals) {
  String result = "";
  for (Rental rental : rentals)
    result += String.format(
      "%s%s%s\n",
      startsWith,
      rental.getLineItem(),
      endsWith);
  return result;
}

public static String expStatement(
  String formatStr,
  Customer customer,
  String rentalInfo) {
  return String.format(
    formatStr,
    customer.getName(),
    rentalInfo,
    customer.getTotalCharge(),
    customer.getTotalPoints());
}
}
```

Expecting Literals

```
public class CustomerTest {
  @Test
  public void statementFor1Rental() {
    Customer customer =
      a.customer.w(
        mock(Rental.class)).build();

    assertEquals(
      "Rental record for Jim\n" +
      "\tnull\n" +
      "Amount owed is 0.0\n" +
      "You earned 0 frequent renter points",
      customer.statement());
  }

  @Test
  public void statementFor2Rentals() {
    Customer customer =
      a.customer.w(
        mock(Rental.class),
        mock(Rental.class)).build();

    assertEquals(
      "Rental record for Jim\n"+
      "\tnull\n" +
      "\tnull\n" +
      "Amount owed is 0.0\n" +
      "You earned 0 frequent renter points",
      customer.statement());
  }
}
```

Which of the previous `CustomerTest` classes would you prefer to maintain?

Negative Testing

It seems that every test suite eventually contains some number of what I call Negative Tests: tests that assert something did **not** happen. These tests can live in various forms, both *State Verification* and *Behavior Verification*. The following tests represent some of the most common patterns.

```java
public class RentalTest {
  @Test
  public void
  storeMockNeverReceivesRemove() {
    Movie movie = mock(Movie.class);
    Rental rental =
      a.rental.w(movie).build();
    Store store = mock(Store.class);
    when(
      store.getAvailability(
        any(Movie.class)))
      .thenReturn(0);
    rental.start(store);
    verify(store, never()).remove(movie);
  }


  @Test
  public void failOnStoreRemove() {
    Movie movie = mock(Movie.class);
    Rental rental =
      a.rental.w(movie).build();
    Store store = new Store(
      new HashMap<Movie,Integer>()) {
        public void remove(Movie movie) {
          fail();
        }
      };
    rental.start(store);
  }
```

```
@Test
public void storeShouldNeverRemove() {
  final boolean[] removeCalled = { false };
  Movie movie = mock(Movie.class);
  Rental rental =
    a.rental.w(movie).build();
  Store store = new Store(
    new HashMap<Movie,Integer>()) {
      public void remove(Movie movie) {
        removeCalled[0] = true;
      }
    };
  rental.start(store);
  assertFalse(removeCalled[0]);
  }
}
```

Where to begin? The first example is probably the most reasonable of the group; though, it has some major flaws. We'll come back to that. The second example is not a *Solitary Unit Test* (uses 2 concrete classes), and violates the Assert Last principle. The third example is also a *Sociable Unit Test*, but at least it follows *Assert Last*. Still, no one actually believes the final + Array trick is the best solution, do they?

The largest flaw is shared by all 3 tests: if the implementation of Rental.start changes, e.g. by calling an overloaded version of remove that also takes a quantity, none of these three tests will fail. This is always the largest problem with negative testing: they guarantee that something didn't happen, but they make no guarantee that the system is integrating as desired.

I'm not sure there's ever much value in these dubious tests; however, if you must write something similar there are ways to get more value than the above examples provide.

Strict Mocking

In general I believe Strict Mocking creates brittle tests and should be avoided. Nonetheless, if you find yourself in need of a negative test, your best bet may be to verify exactly what did and did not happen during execution. The following test ensures that getAvailability was called with a specific movie, and no other interactions occurred with store.

```java
public class RentalTest {
  @Test
  public void verifyStoreInteractions() {
    Movie movie = mock(Movie.class);
    Rental rental =
      a.rental.w(movie).build();
    Store store = mock(Store.class);
    rental.start(store);
    verify(store).getAvailability(movie);
    verifyNoMoreInteractions(store);
  }
}
```

Just Be Sociable

The test above is currently passing, and ensures that any interactions with store in the future will cause a failing test. The test violates One Assertion Per Test, but that's not actually what bothers me the most. I find myself asking: what value is this test actually providing me?

What if the implementation of Rental.start changes and the only interaction with store is the call to getAvailability? We'll have code that simultaneously provides no value and provides no indication that it should be deleted. What if the implementation of Store changes in a way where a call to remove would be perfectly reasonable?

The entire point of this test is to verify reasonable integration between Store and Rental. Why not simply test what's important in a *Sociable Unit Test*? In fact, we're already testing the integration of Store and Rental in a previously seen Rental *Sociable Unit Test*. Below is the updated version, which contains the test you've previously seen, and a new test that ensures store.getAvailability continues to work as expected for the case where a movie has no availability.

```
public class RentalTest {
  @Test
  public void
  storeAvailabilityIsModifiedOnRental() {
    Movie movie = a.movie.build();
    Rental rental =
      a.rental.w(movie).build();
    Store store =
      a.store.w(movie, movie).build();
    rental.start(store);
    a.rental.build().start(store);
    assertEquals(
      1, store.getAvailability(movie));
  }

  @Test
  public void
  storeAvailabilityIsUnmodified() {
    Movie movie = a.movie.build();
    Rental rental =
      a.rental.w(movie).build();
    Store store = a.store.build();
    rental.start(store);
    assertEquals(
      0, store.getAvailability(movie));
  }
}
```

The above *Sociable Unit Test* removes the need for any of the previously written negative tests. This is yet another example of the value of asking ourselves '*why?*'.

I began by asking '*why is it hard to get positive ROI out of this test?'*, which led me to '*why am I testing this interaction in the first place?'*. Answering that question led me to a test that both covers the desired functionality and is easier to maintain in the long term.

Hamcrest

You may find Hamcrest[16] to be conspicuously absent from
this chapter. In theory I like many things about Hamcrest
matchers, in practice I never seem to use them within my test
suites. My theory and practice are a bit at odds, thus I neither
advocate for nor discourage the use of Hamcrest.

---

[16]http://hamcrest.org/

Improving Test Cases

In order to have an effective test suite you must have maintainable test cases; unfortunately, seldom does a team agree on which patterns will produce maintainable test cases.

Many talented engineers believe maintainable test cases contain no duplication and follow common object oriented abstractions. Others, such as myself, contend that applying DRY and OO patterns to independently executing procedural programs (tests) decreases readability.

Tests are procedural by nature. Allowing developers to read tests in a procedural manner would be the natural choice, yet it's rarely possible.

The original xUnit frameworks were written using (early versions of) Java, thus classes and methods were the only reasonable choices for creating test cases and individual tests. Still, I find it interesting that writing procedural code using an OO language is considered terrible design, and no one gives a second thought to writing procedural tests using OO constructs.

Within domain code:

- The primary motivation for naming a method is the ability to call it.
- Instance methods collaborate to produce a running application.
- Instance methods share instance variables.

Within test code:

- The primary motivation for naming a test method is documentation; calling a test method explicitly is an anti-pattern.
- Instance method collaboration is considered an anti-pattern.
- Each instance method is magically given its own set of instance variables.

Every programmer new to testing must learn that traditional OO concepts may directly conflict with how they must now read and write tests.

JUnit remains tied to the classic testing pattern of classes for test cases and methods for individual tests. Despite this design choice, it's valuable to remember the following.

- Tests are procedural.
- Each test method should encapsulate the entire lifecycle and verification, independent of other test methods.
- Tests methods should have very specific goals which can be easily identified by maintainers.

While we are forced to use an OO language for our procedural tests, no one forces us to follow OO patterns.

When it comes to test cases, I define maintainability as: when a test breaks, what can it contain that will simplify finding the fix? The rest of this chapter details what tools I use to be maximally effective.

Too Much Magic

Almost every test suite contains a failed experiment that ought to be deleted. The following subsections are examples of failed experiments that need to be replaced.

Self-shunt

I hate to pick on a paper[17] written by Michael Feathers after he was kind enough to write the foreword and bless the title of this book. That said, I can't get behind the use of Self-shunt (and I suspect Michael would likely agree at this point). The basic idea of Self-shunt is to pass the Test Case instance as a collaborator to collect data that you'll later use for verification.

An example is worth a thousand words. Below is an example of using a Self-shunt to verify the interaction between Store and Rental.

---

[17]http://www.objectmentor.com/resources/articles/SelfShunPtrn.pdf

```java
public class RentalTest extends Store {
  public static Movie movie =
    mock(Movie.class);
  private boolean removeCalled;

  public RentalTest() {
    super(new HashMap<Movie, Integer>() {{
        this.put(movie, 2);
      }});
  }

  @Test
  public void removeIsCalled() {
    Rental rental =
      a.rental.w(movie).build();
    rental.start(this);
    assertEquals(true, removeCalled);
  }

  public void remove(Movie movie) {
    super.remove(movie);
    removeCalled = true;
  }
}
```

That's quite a test. Like Michael, I'm guilty of trying this
pattern[18] out at one point as well. In theory it seemed like
a clever idea. You want to test collaboration, why not use a
class instance that's immediately relevant? Hopefully the test
above demonstrates *exactly why not.*

---

[18]http://blog.jayfields.com/2005/04/tasc-unit-testing-pattern.html

Much of the code required for this clever implementation does not easily convey its purpose.

- The constructor is complicated for no immediately obvious reason. Test cases rarely have constructors, much less constructors calling super with domain objects.
- The remove method is obviously a helper method, but it's neither explicitly called nor otherwise explained.
- Passing a test case to a domain method would surely be jarring to someone unfamiliar with this pattern.
- The removeCalled boolean lives divorced from the assertions where it's relevant.
- Were this not a book example, other tests would live in here as well, all of which wouldn't care about the crazy constructor, the static Movie mock, or the removeCalled boolean.

To put it mildly, there's too much magic here; this implementation is so clever it forces the reader to deeply understand an individual test, the entire test case, and how the testing framework is implemented.

I applaud people who experiment in this way; however, surely a mock would be a better choice in this instance. If you find *clever* code like the above example, do not hesitate to replace the magic with something more explicit.

Exceptional Success

There's another example of too much magic that I want to briefly mention: using an exception to indicate success.

Let's say you're looking to test the same remove method as the previous example. You want to write a test that ensures the remove method is called, but you don't want to introduce a capturing array such as the one we previously saw in *Negative Testing*.

The following test fulfills your requirements.

```java
public class RentalTest {
  @Test(expected=RuntimeException.class)
  public void removeIsCalled() {
    final Movie movie = mock(Movie.class);
    Rental rental =
      a.rental.w(movie).build();
    HashMap<Movie, Integer> movieMap =
      new HashMap<Movie, Integer>() {{
        this.put(movie, 2);
      }};
    Store store =
      new Store(movieMap) {
        public void remove(Movie movie) {
          throw new
            RuntimeException("success");
        }
      };
    rental.start(store);
  }
}
```

If you laughed when you read that test, you're not alone. Those are the kinds of tests that I appreciate as someone who likes to bend languages to my will. That said, there's unquestionably too much magic in that test. If you find a test similar to that within your test suite, do the team a favor and refactor to verifying a mock interaction.

I could probably write an entire book on tests with too much magic, but hopefully these 2 examples get the point across. Clever tests are fun to write and enjoyable from a language geek perspective; however, they have no place in a test suite maintained by a team looking to deliver effectively.

Inline Setup

Setup is a special method within a test case that runs before each test. Setup was traditionally implemented using the Template Method pattern; however, the latest versions of JUnit allow you to define a Setup method using the `@Before` annotation. The current JUnit documentation states the following:

> When writing tests, it is common to find that several tests need similar objects created before they can run.

I'll freely admit that Setup can reduce character duplication; unfortunately, it's often at the expense of readability.

If you aspire to create tiny universes with minimal conceptual overhead, rarely will you find the opportunity to use Setup. To begin with, if you were to pretend that the universe you're currently working with was the first and only, it would be hard to justify creating a setup method that divorced creation from verification. Even when you view your test case as a whole, Setup becomes hard to justify once it contains any data that is used in a subset of the tests.

The cost (in terms of understanding) of a Setup method is the sum of understanding each object created and action performed. The value of a Setup method, viewed from the test level, would be each instantiation or action that no longer needs to exist in the test itself. The waste could then be defined as the sum of each unnecessary instantiation, each unnecessary action, and the cost of indirection. To be clear, I'm unconcerned with the computing resources wasted; I believe Setup is a negative ROI pattern based on the wasted programmer time.

Below you'll find a test that demonstrates pushing all creation logic into Setup. A real CustomerTest should also include tests for zero and one rental Customer instances as well, I left them out for the sake of brevity.

```java
public class CustomerTest {
  Rental godfatherRental;
  Rental lionKingRental;
  Rental scarfaceRental;
  Rental notebookRental;
  Customer twoRentals;
  Customer fourRentals;

  @Before
  public void init() {
    godfatherRental = mock(Rental.class);
    when(godfatherRental.getTitle())
      .thenReturn("Godfather 4");
    when(godfatherRental.getCharge())
      .thenReturn(3.0);
    when(godfatherRental.getPoints())
      .thenReturn(2);
    lionKingRental = mock(Rental.class);
    when(lionKingRental.getTitle())
      .thenReturn("Lion King");
    when(lionKingRental.getCharge())
      .thenReturn(2.0);
    when(lionKingRental.getPoints())
      .thenReturn(1);
    scarfaceRental = mock(Rental.class);
```

```
when(scarfaceRental.getTitle())
  .thenReturn("Scarface");
when(scarfaceRental.getCharge())
  .thenReturn(1.0);
when(scarfaceRental.getPoints())
  .thenReturn(1);
notebookRental = mock(Rental.class);
when(notebookRental.getTitle())
  .thenReturn("Notebook");
when(notebookRental.getCharge())
  .thenReturn(6.0);
when(notebookRental.getPoints())
  .thenReturn(1);

twoRentals =
  a.customer.w(
    godfatherRental, lionKingRental)
  .build();

fourRentals =
  a.customer.w(
    godfatherRental, lionKingRental,
    scarfaceRental, notebookRental)
  .build();
}
```

```java
@Test
public void recentRentalsWith2Rentals() {
  assertEquals(
    "Recent rentals:"+
    "\nGodfather 4\nLion King",
    twoRentals.recentRentals());
}

@Test
public void recentRentalsWith4Rentals() {
  assertEquals(
    "Recent rentals:"+
    "\nGodfather 4\nLion King\nScarface",
    fourRentals.recentRentals());
}

@Test
public void totalChargeWith2Rentals() {
  assertEquals(
    5.0,
    twoRentals.getTotalCharge(),
    0);
}

@Test
public void totalChargeWith4Rentals() {
  assertEquals(
    12.0,
    fourRentals.getTotalCharge(),
    0);
}
```

```java
@Test
public void totalPointsWith2Rentals() {
  assertEquals(
    3,
    twoRentals.getTotalPoints());
}

@Test
public void totalPointsWith4Rentals() {
  assertEquals(
    5,
    fourRentals.getTotalPoints());
}

@Test
public void getName() {
  assertEquals(
    "Jim", twoRentals.getName());
}
}
```

Here's the cost of Setup from the previous example:

- godfatherRental is a mock Rental
  - that returns the "Godfather 4" from getTitle
  - that returns 3.0 from getCharge
  - that returns 2 from getPoints
- lionKingRental is a mock Rental
  - that returns the "Lion King" from getTitle
  - that returns 2.0 from getCharge
  - that returns 1 from getPoints
- scarfaceRental is a mock Rental
  - that returns the "Scarface" from getTitle
  - that returns 1.0 from getCharge
  - that returns 1 from getPoints
- notebookRental is a mock Rental
  - that returns the "Notebook" from getTitle
  - that returns 6.0 from getCharge
  - that returns 1 from getPoints
- twoRentals is a Customer with godfatherRental and lionKingRental
- fourRentals is a Customer with godfatherRental, lionKingRental, scarfaceRental, and notebookRental

The value per test varies based on the assertion, but it's safe to say no test contains zero waste. It would be unreasonable to discuss the value and waste from every test, but I would like to look briefly at one or two of them.

The following is the cost breakdown for Setup for the
`totalChargeWith2Rentals` test.

Value

- godfatherRental is a mock `Rental`
  - that returns 3.0 from `getCharge`
- lionKingRental is a mock `Rental`
  - that returns 2.0 from `getCharge`
- twoRentals is a Customer with `godfatherRental` and
  `lionKingRental`

Waste

- godfatherRental
  - that returns the "Godfather 4" from `getTitle`
  - that returns 2 from `getPoints`
- lionKingRental
  - that returns the "Lion King" from `getTitle`
  - that returns 1 from `getPoints`
- scarfaceRental is a mock `Rental`
  - that returns the "Scarface" from `getTitle`
  - that returns 1.0 from `getCharge`
  - that returns 1 from `getPoints`
- notebookRental is a mock `Rental`
  - that returns the "Notebook" from `getTitle`
  - that returns 6.0 from `getCharge`
  - that returns 1 from `getPoints`
- fourRentals is a Customer with `godfatherRental`,
  `lionKingRental`, `scarfaceRental`, and `notebookRental`

Imagine the same list for getName.

Advocates of Setup argue that you need only pay the *under-standing cost* once. I contend it's much more likely that you'll pay it once per encounter with CustomerTest. It's likely that you'll have flushed the understanding between interactions with the CustomerTest class. Even if you remember the details the *Setup* will surely change at some point, forcing you to reacquaint yourself with the logic.

I would also contend that the most common interaction with these tests will be dealing with a failing test or two. In that situation you'll be forced to understand all of Setup, with the actual value derived from Setup likely being very small for the failing tests that you're looking to fix.

Similar Creation and Action

A primary argument for Setup is reducing creation duplica-tion. As I've shown throughout this book, I prefer to reduce creation duplication by introducing globally used builders. The domain objects I've been building are admittedly straight-forward. Faced with the Setup vs Builder decision some use the excuse that their domain objects cannot be easily built. When I hear this argument I like to repeat the following quote.

> Where there's smoke, pour gasoline –Scott Con-ley

Duplicate code is a smell. Setup and Teardown are deodorant, but they don't fix the underlying issue. Using a Setup method is basically like hiding your junk in the closet. Refactoring to a domain that allows easy use of Builders is a **solution**.

Obviousness

Another reason I like to avoid Setup is the complete lack of transparency. If you look at all of the tests from the last example, in none of them can you find code that says *go look at Setup to get a better idea of what's going on here.* If you open the code to a failing test and the Setup is off screen, there are zero clues indicating the existence of a Setup.

At best, this is inconvenient; things go downhill quickly from there. I once opened a test case that had several tests which were dependent on a Setup method. Additionally, the test case contained another group of tests that used a private method for initialization. The logic in the private method was almost a perfect duplicate of the logic in the Setup. Clearly one author didn't notice the existing creation solution and, in their attempt to be DRY, duplicated exactly what was already available.

Setup As An Optimization

Many developers justify using Setup as a solution to their speed problems. For example, it's unquestionably true that creating a database connection per *Sociable Unit Test* would be slower than creating one in each test within a single *Test Case.* That said, why are we creating more than one database connection at all? Why not create one global connection and run each test in a transaction that's automatically rolled back after each *Sociable Unit Test*?

The above example is a specific case of using Setup to hide a problem that could be unhidden and solved by spending the time to find a global solution. I've run into this type of problem for as long as I've been applying *Inline Setup* to

Sociable Unit Tests. Deleting numerous files with Java is slow: True. Shelling out and deleting the parent directory is fast: True. Loading a large data set through a Java SQL lib is slow: True. Bulk loading a database using command line tools is fast: True.

When I find that execution of my *Sociable Unit Tests* is growing too slow, I take the time to answer the following questions:

- Are all the *Sociable Unit Tests* still necessary?
- Are the interactions with the File System, Database, and/or Messaging System still necessary?
- Is there a faster way to accomplish any of the tasks setting the File System, Database and/or Messaging System back to a known state?

Using a Setup is the easy answer, but it's also the selfish answer. When faced with the choice to force complexity on a teammate in the future or optimize the `Sociable` tests for everyone now, good teammates choose the latter (and admittedly harder) path.

Comparison

Immediately below you'll find the version of `CustomerTest` that we saw earlier in this section. Below that is the same test case written with `Setup` inlined. If you're willing to indulge me, pretend you don't know what's going on in the `Setup` method and you're looking into why `totalChargeWith2Rentals` is failing. Read `totalChargeWith2Rentals` and the `Setup` immediately below first, then look at the same method in the

2nd `CustomerTest` and decide which you'd rather encounter during your work day.

(do the same for the `getName` test if you'd like extra emphasis)

With Setup

```java
public class CustomerTest {
  Rental godfatherRental;
  Rental lionKingRental;
  Rental scarfaceRental;
  Rental notebookRental;
  Customer twoRentals;
  Customer fourRentals;

  @Before
  public void init() {
    godfatherRental = mock(Rental.class);
    when(godfatherRental.getTitle())
      .thenReturn("Godfather 4");
    when(godfatherRental.getCharge())
      .thenReturn(3.0);
    when(godfatherRental.getPoints())
      .thenReturn(2);
    lionKingRental = mock(Rental.class);
    when(lionKingRental.getTitle())
      .thenReturn("Lion King");
    when(lionKingRental.getCharge())
      .thenReturn(2.0);
    when(lionKingRental.getPoints())
      .thenReturn(1);
    scarfaceRental = mock(Rental.class);
    when(scarfaceRental.getTitle())
```

```
    .thenReturn("Scarface");
when(scarfaceRental.getCharge())
    .thenReturn(1.0);
when(scarfaceRental.getPoints())
    .thenReturn(1);
notebookRental = mock(Rental.class);
when(notebookRental.getTitle())
    .thenReturn("Notebook");
when(notebookRental.getCharge())
    .thenReturn(6.0);
when(notebookRental.getPoints())
    .thenReturn(1);

twoRentals =
    a.customer.w(
        godfatherRental, lionKingRental)
    .build();

fourRentals =
    a.customer.w(
        godfatherRental, lionKingRental,
        scarfaceRental, notebookRental)
    .build();
}
```

```java
@Test
public void recentRentalsWith2Rentals() {
  assertEquals(
    "Recent rentals:"+
    "\nGodfather 4\nLion King",
    twoRentals.recentRentals());
}

@Test
public void recentRentalsWith4Rentals() {
  assertEquals(
    "Recent rentals:"+
    "\nGodfather 4\nLion King\nScarface",
    fourRentals.recentRentals());
}

@Test
public void totalChargeWith2Rentals() {
  assertEquals(
    5.0,
    twoRentals.getTotalCharge(),
    0);
}

@Test
public void totalChargeWith4Rentals() {
  assertEquals(
    12.0,
    fourRentals.getTotalCharge(),
    0);
}
```

```java
@Test
public void totalPointsWith2Rentals() {
  assertEquals(
    3,
    twoRentals.getTotalPoints());
}

@Test
public void totalPointsWith4Rentals() {
  assertEquals(
    5,
    fourRentals.getTotalPoints());
}

@Test
public void getName() {
  assertEquals(
    "Jim", twoRentals.getName());
}
}
```

Without Setup

```java
public class CustomerTest {
  @Test
  public void recentRentalsWith2Rentals() {
    Rental godfatherRental =
      mock(Rental.class);
    when(godfatherRental.getTitle())
      .thenReturn("Godfather 4");
    Rental lionKingRental =
      mock(Rental.class);
    when(lionKingRental.getTitle())
      .thenReturn("Lion King");
    assertEquals(
      "Recent rentals:"+
      "\nGodfather 4\nLion King",
      a.customer.w(
        godfatherRental, lionKingRental)
      .build().recentRentals());
  }
```

```
@Test
public void recentRentalsWith4Rentals() {
  Rental godfatherRental =
    mock(Rental.class);
  when(godfatherRental.getTitle())
    .thenReturn("Godfather 4");
  Rental lionKingRental =
    mock(Rental.class);
  when(lionKingRental.getTitle())
    .thenReturn("Lion King");
  Rental scarfaceRental =
    mock(Rental.class);
  when(scarfaceRental.getTitle())
    .thenReturn("Scarface");
  Rental notebookRental =
    mock(Rental.class);
  when(notebookRental.getTitle())
    .thenReturn("Notebook");
  assertEquals(
    "Recent rentals:"+
    "\nGodfather 4\nLion King\nScarface",
    a.customer.w(
      godfatherRental, lionKingRental,
      scarfaceRental, notebookRental)
    .build().recentRentals());
}
```

```
@Test
public void totalChargeWith2Rentals() {
  Rental godfatherRental =
    mock(Rental.class);
  when(godfatherRental.getCharge())
    .thenReturn(3.0);
  Rental lionKingRental =
    mock(Rental.class);
  when(lionKingRental.getCharge())
    .thenReturn(2.0);
  assertEquals(
    5.0,
    a.customer.w(
      godfatherRental, lionKingRental)
    .build().getTotalCharge(),
    0);
}
```

```
@Test
public void totalChargeWith4Rentals() {
  Rental godfatherRental =
    mock(Rental.class);
  when(godfatherRental.getCharge())
    .thenReturn(3.0);
  Rental lionKingRental =
    mock(Rental.class);
  when(lionKingRental.getCharge())
    .thenReturn(2.0);
  Rental scarfaceRental =
    mock(Rental.class);
  when(scarfaceRental.getCharge())
    .thenReturn(1.0);
  Rental notebookRental =
    mock(Rental.class);
  when(notebookRental.getCharge())
    .thenReturn(6.0);
  assertEquals(
    12.0,
    a.customer.w(
      godfatherRental, lionKingRental,
      scarfaceRental, notebookRental)
    .build().getTotalCharge(),
    0);
}
```

```java
@Test
public void totalPointsWith2Rentals() {
  Rental godfatherRental =
    mock(Rental.class);
  when(godfatherRental.getPoints())
    .thenReturn(2);
  Rental lionKingRental =
    mock(Rental.class);
  when(lionKingRental.getPoints())
    .thenReturn(1);
  assertEquals(
    3,
    a.customer.w(
      godfatherRental, lionKingRental)
    .build().getTotalPoints());
}
```

```java
@Test
public void totalPointsWith4Rentals() {
  Rental godfatherRental =
    mock(Rental.class);
  when(godfatherRental.getPoints())
    .thenReturn(2);
  Rental lionKingRental =
    mock(Rental.class);
  when(lionKingRental.getPoints())
    .thenReturn(1);
  Rental scarfaceRental =
    mock(Rental.class);
  when(scarfaceRental.getPoints())
    .thenReturn(1);
  Rental notebookRental =
    mock(Rental.class);
  when(notebookRental.getPoints())
    .thenReturn(1);
  assertEquals(
    5,
    a.customer.w(
      godfatherRental, lionKingRental,
      scarfaceRental, notebookRental)
    .build().getTotalPoints());
}
```

```
@Test
public void getName() {
  assertEquals(
    "Jim",
    a.customer.build().getName());
  }
}
```

Test Names

Two previous statements that remain true:

- JUnit tests are implemented as methods, thus a method name is required.
- I'm not a fan of test names.

Another truth: *Test names are glorified comments*

> A method selector is always necessary to refer to the method from other places. Not necessarily a name, but some kind of selector is needed. That's not true for test names, and to a degree it's interesting that the default of having test names comes from the implementation artifact of tests usually being represented as methods. Would we still have test names in all cases if we didn't start designing a test framework based around a language that cripples usage of abstractions other than methods for executable code? –Ola Bini

People rarely think about test names in that way, but at the end of the day they're merely (at best) a description of what the test is verifying. A **required** description.

I tend to agree with the following discussion of comments.

> Don't worry, we aren't saying that people shouldn't write comments. In our olfactory analogy, comments aren't a bad smell; indeed they are a sweet

> smell. The reason we mention comments here is
> that comments often are used as a deodorant.
> It's surprising how often you look at thickly
> commented code and notice that the comments
> are there because the code is bad. –Fowler &
> Beck, Refactoring

Once I recognized that test names were comments I began to look at them differently. I wondered if all of the concerns with comments could also be applied to test names.

Refactoring goes on to say the following about comments:

> Comments lead us to bad code that has all the
> rotten whiffs we've discussed in [Chapter 3 of
> Refactoring]. Our first action is to remove the bad
> smells by refactoring. When we're finished, we
> often find that the comments are superfluous.

While it may not be possible to delete test names entirely, I believe it's absolutely worth making them superfluous. I've found that refactoring the domain in a way that encourages *tests that would be self-explanatory without a name* benefits both other tests and the domain code itself.

Refactoring also provides guidance on how to change the domain model.

> If you need a comment to explain what a block
> of code does, try Extract Method. If the method is
> already extracted but you still need a comment to
> explain what it does, use Rename Method. If you
> need to state some rules about the required state
> of the system, use Introduce Assertion.

To be clear, I don't think you should be extracting or renaming methods in your tests, I think test names can indicate that those things are needed in the code you are testing. Conversely, Introduce Assertion could apply directly to your test. Instead of stating your assumptions in the test name, introduce an assertion that verifies an assumption. Or better yet, break the larger test up into several smaller tests that abide by One Assertion Per Test.

While reviewing this book Graham Nash posed the following question.

> When a test or tests break, do you not find the list of broken names that JUnit outputs to be useful? What would be there instead if you could have anonymous methods?

I do not. To quote Ron Jeffries *"Code never lies, comments sometimes do".* When a test is broken I'm rarely interested in what the test should be doing, I want to know what the test is actually doing. My only use for the JUnit failure output was to navigate to the test.

Were I able to create anonymous tests, failure output would include the test definition file name and line number rather than a test name. I've used this pattern extensively in both Ruby and Clojure (where anonymous tests are possible) and never run into trouble finding or sharing a pointer to a specific test.

It's also important to note that using a test framework that promotes anonymous tests does not prohibit you from adding a description as a comment. Well written test names often tell you *why* a test exists, and it's valuable to continue to capture that data as a comment associated with the test. On the other hand, test names that describe *how* are often perfect candidates for anonymous tests with no associated comment.

I've clearly digressed from the main point: There's no reasonable way (that I'm aware of) to write anonymous tests in JUnit; still, it's always worth taking at least one look at your test and asking yourself *If this test had no name, would it convey my intent?*

Improving Test Suites

In the Motivators chapter I repeatedly recommend deleting tests that no longer provide positive ROI. While I believe this to be an essential activity, I also believe an attempt to create positive ROI from an existing test is an equally essential prerequisite.

Separating The Solitary From The Sociable

Chapter 3 defines *Solitary* and *Sociable Unit Tests*, and provides the first examples of converting *Sociable Unit Tests* to *Solitary*. Chapter 4 provides additional guidance on *how* to create *Solitary Unit Tests*. Now that you know *how* to create *Solitary Unit Tests* you might be wondering "*why?*".

There are two primary reasons for writing *Solitary Unit Tests*:

1. *Sociable Unit Tests* can be slow and nondeterministic
2. *Sociable Unit Tests* are more susceptible to cascading failures

Increasing Consistency And Speed With Solitary Unit Tests

Impurity is the nemesis of test repeatability. Crossing boundaries is the nemesis of test speed. If every method you wrote were pure, you'd have a hard time creating flaky tests or slow tests. Unfortunately, that's not the world that most of us live in. The following bullets are the three most common ways to increase the fragility and execution time of your test suite.

- interacting with a database
- interacting with the filesystem
- interacting with time

Database and Filesystem Interaction

In most languages it's common to use either a standard library or a commonly used library for database and filesystem access. The APIs of these libraries are often defined for ease of use within your object model; however, the ability to write *Solitary Unit Tests* is not often supported. For that reason, I always recommend wrapping the commonly used libraries with a gateway that provides the following capabilities:

- the ability to disallow access within *Solitary Unit Tests*
- the ability to reset to a base state before each *Sociable Unit Test.*

The guidelines above are simple enough; however, I think an example might make clear exactly what I'm looking for. Let's assume I have the following class that I'd like to test.

```
public class PidWriter {
  public static void writePid(
    String filename,
    RuntimeMXBean bean) {
    try {
      writePidtoFile(filename, bean);
    } catch (IOException e) {
      throw new RuntimeException(e);
    }
  }

  private static void writePidtoFile(
    String filename,
    RuntimeMXBean bean) throws IOException {
    FileWriter writer =
      new FileWriter(filename);
    try {
      String runtimeName = bean.getName();
      writer.write(
        runtimeName.substring(
          0, runtimeName.indexOf('@')));
    }
    finally {
      writer.close();
    }
  }
}
```

The following test does the trick, but it's not what I would consider to be well written.

```
public class PidWriterTest {
  @Test
  public void writePid() throws Exception {
    RuntimeMXBean bean =
      mock(RuntimeMXBean.class);
    when(bean.getName()).thenReturn("12@X");
    PidWriter.writePid(
      "/tmp/sample.pid", bean);
    assertEquals(
      "12",
      Files.readAllLines(
        Paths.get("/tmp/sample.pid"),
        Charset.defaultCharset()).get(0));
  }
}
```

Any number of issues could cause false negatives or positives, e.g. If the `PidWriter` contains a bug and a previously saved `sample.pid` file exists, the assertion will continue to pass. Likewise, if the `sample.pid` file is overwritten by some other process mid-test, the test will fail despite `PidWriter` working as expected.

The Solitary Unit Test

The first change I would make would be to refactor towards a `PidWriter` *Solitary Unit Test*. As I said above, when working with classes like `FileWriter` I like to create my own gateway that can disallow access within the *Solitary Unit Tests*.

```
public class FileWriterGateway
  extends FileWriter {

  public static boolean disallowAccess =
    false;

  public FileWriterGateway(
    String filename) throws IOException {
    super(filename);
    if (disallowAccess) {
      throw new RuntimeException(
        "access disallowed");
    }
  }
}
```

Below you can see the switch in PidWriter to use FileWriterGateway.

```
public class PidWriter {
  public static void writePid(
    String filename,
    RuntimeMXBean bean) {
    try {
      writePidtoFile(filename, bean);
    } catch (IOException e) {
      throw new RuntimeException(e);
    }
  }

  private static void writePidtoFile(
    String filename,
    RuntimeMXBean bean) throws IOException {
    FileWriterGateway writer =
      new FileWriterGateway(filename);
    try {
      String runtimeName = bean.getName();
      writer.write(
        runtimeName.substring(
          0, runtimeName.indexOf('@')));
    }
    finally {
      writer.close();
    }
  }
}
```

Finally, running the PidWriterTest below will result in the immediately following failure.

```java
public class PidWriterTest extends Solitary {
  @Test
  public void writePid() throws Exception {
    RuntimeMXBean bean =
      mock(RuntimeMXBean.class);
    when(bean.getName()).thenReturn("12@X");
    PidWriter.writePid(
      "/tmp/sample.pid", bean);
    assertEquals(
      "12",
      Files.readAllLines(
        Paths.get("/tmp/sample.pid"),
        Charset.defaultCharset()).get(0));
  }
}
```

```
JUnit version 4.11
.E
There was 1 failure:
1) writePid(PidWriterTest)
java.lang.RuntimeException: access disallowed

FAILURES!!!
Tests run: 1,  Failures: 1
```

If you looked closely at the PidWriterTest you likely noticed that the only change between the last two versions is the addition of extends Solitary in the latter.

You shouldn't have any desire to remember to repeat a call to disallowAccess where necessary; however, a simple rule such as *all tests in a solitary package should extend Solitary* is both easy to remember and automatically verify.

The implementation of Solitary might surprise you.

```
public class Solitary {
  @Before
  public void setup() {
    FileWriterGateway.disallowAccess = true;
  }
}
```

It may appear hypocritical that I would spend an entire section (and some) denouncing setup, only to recommend it in a later chapter. However, I believe this example demonstrates exactly the type of refactoring that I've previously recommended: *solve problems locally and globally, exclusively.*

While the PidWriterTest is the first usage you've seen of Solitary, in an actual codebase I would enforce extend Solitary within each *Solitary Unit Test*. This strict conformance would give me a single place to put all *disallowing* code as well as give me globally applicable understanding and confidence, i.e. all *Solitary Unit Tests* disallow the same things, and I'm confident that all disallowed things are being prevented in each *Solitary Unit Test.*

Now that Solitary and FileWriterGateway are collaborating to ensure proper *Solitary Unit Testing*, it's time to change the PidWriterTest and get it passing.

There's no easy way to write a *Solitary Unit Test* for PidWriter as it stands; however, an overload of the existing public method allows us to write the following.

```
public class PidWriterTest extends Solitary {
  @Test
  public void writePid() throws Exception {
    RuntimeMXBean bean =
      mock(RuntimeMXBean.class);
    when(bean.getName()).thenReturn("12@X");
    FileWriterGateway facade =
      mock(FileWriterGateway.class);
    PidWriter.writePid(facade, bean);
    verify(facade).write("12");
  }
}
```

The new PidWriter (that includes the overloaded method
we're testing) can be found below.

```
public class PidWriter {
  public static void writePid(
    String filename,
    RuntimeMXBean bean) {
    try {
      FileWriterGateway writer =
        new FileWriterGateway(filename);
      writePid(writer, bean);
    } catch (IOException e) {
      throw new RuntimeException(e);
    }
  }

  public static void writePid(
    FileWriterGateway facade,
    RuntimeMXBean bean) {
    try {
      writePidtoFile(facade, bean);
    } catch (IOException e) {
      throw new RuntimeException(e);
    }
  }
```

```
private static void writePidtoFile(
  FileWriterGateway facade,
  RuntimeMXBean bean) throws IOException {
  try {
    String runtimeName = bean.getName();
    facade.write(
      runtimeName.substring(
        0, runtimeName.indexOf('@')));
  } catch (IOException e) {
    throw new RuntimeException(e);
  }
  finally {
    facade.close();
  }
}
}
```

While reviewing this book Jake McCrary posed the following question.

> Why overload the public method rather than exposing the private method?

When I'm introducing a method strictly to allow *Solitary Unit Testing* I like to take the following steps.

1. Copy the original method.
2. Call the copied method from the original method.
3. Move anything hampering *Solitary Unit Testing* back to the original method.

By following those steps I ensure that my *Solitary Unit Test* is able to verify as much behavior as possible. In most cases the copied method will contain enough behavior to justify its existence, in the previous example it's debatable. As written, our tests can ignore the `IOException` thrown by `writePidToFile`; however, I also think it would be perfectly reasonable to instead expose the private method and handle the `IOException` within the test. In practice I would follow the above steps to see the result, then decide which implementation I found more maintainable.

The final *Solitary* `PidWriterTest` provides me confidence that `PidWriter` is delegating to `FileWriterGateway` as desired. In most cases, this will be the only positive ROI test for `PidWriter`.

The Sociable Unit Test

Sociable Unit Tests with side effects (writing to a file, database, messaging system) are often orders of magnitude slower and orders of magnitude more fragile; these factors must be taken into account when determining ROI. Still, there will be times when the functionality is important enough that a *Sociable Unit Test* will be justified.

Were the `PidWriter` important enough to warrant *Sociable Unit Tests*, I would write a test along the lines of the following.

```
public class PidWriterTest extends Sociable {
  @Test
  public void writePid() throws Exception {
    RuntimeMXBean bean =
      mock(RuntimeMXBean.class);
    when(bean.getName()).thenReturn("12@X");
    PidWriter.writePid(
      "/tmp/wewut/sample.pid", bean);
    assertEquals(
      "12",
      Files.readAllLines(
        Paths.get("/tmp/wewut/sample.pid"),
        Charset.defaultCharset()).get(0));
  }
}
```

The above *Sociable* PidWriterTest uses the writePid(String, RuntimeMxBean) overload, thus reclaiming some test coverage that was lost with in the *Solitary Unit Test*. I suspect it also looks familiar, it's roughly the same as the first test from this (the *Database and Filesystem Interaction*) section. The only notable difference between this and the original test is the extends Sociable directly above. The reasoning for Sociable is largely the same as what was discussed for Solitary; we're more effective if we *always* inherit from one base class that applies consistent constraints to the tests.

In this specific case, my Sociable class is clearing a well known *tmp* dir that's used within *Sociable Unit Tests*.

```
public class Sociable {
  @Before
  public void setup()
    throws Exception {
    Process p;
    p = Runtime.getRuntime().exec(
      "rm -rf /tmp/wewut");
    p.waitFor();
    p = Runtime.getRuntime().exec(
      "mkdir -p /tmp/wewut");
    p.waitFor();
  }
}
```

> note: I chose to shell out for example brevity.
> You'll likely want to use Java classes to manage
> the delete and create if platform independence is
> important to you.

The Sociable class does a good job of cleaning up our
filesystem before each test run. This cleanup obviously comes
at a cost; however, it also provides the benefits of concise tests
and consistent understanding of the state prior to execution -
major advantages.

Revisiting Concerns

I previously expressed concerns about the original test from this section, specifically:

- If the PidWriter contains a bug and a previously saved sample.pid file exists, the assertion will continue to pass.
- If the sample.pid file is overwritten by some other process mid-test, the test will fail despite PidWriter working as expected.

The first concern is completely mitigated by the delete that occurs in the Sociable setup. The second concern can never be completely mitigated; however, the passing *Solitary Unit Test* gives us strong confidence that the code works as expected and the next run of the *Sociable Unit Tests* will likely succeed.

Time Interaction

In theory you could apply the advice from the last subsection to *time* classes as well, though I suspect most people would consider that overkill. If your time library supports freezing at a specific moment, there's an alternative that I consider a pragmatic compromise.

The following Rental class is similar to what we've previously seen, and I've added the concept of creationDateTime. A Rental can be created either with or without a creationDateTime. Rental instances created without a DateTime instance will construct their own creationDateTime within the constructor.

```
public class Rental {

  Movie movie;
  private int daysRented;
  private boolean started;
  private DateTime creationDateTime;

  public Rental(
    Movie movie,
    int daysRented,
    DateTime creationDateTime) {
    this.movie = movie;
    this.daysRented = daysRented;
    this.creationDateTime = creationDateTime;
  }

  public Rental(Movie movie, int daysRented) {
    this(movie, daysRented, new DateTime());
  }

  public DateTime getCreationDateTime() {
    return creationDateTime;
  }
}
```

The tests for these constructors are fairly straightforward:

```
public class RentalTest {
  @Test
  public void creationDateTimeNow() {
    DateTimeUtils.setCurrentMillisFixed(1000);
    Rental rental = a.rental.build();
    assertEquals(
      1000,
      rental.getCreationDateTime()
      .getMillis());
  }

  @Test
  public void creationDateTimeSet() {
    Rental rental =
      a.rental.w(
        new DateTime(199)).build();
    assertEquals(
      199,
      rental.getCreationDateTime()
      .getMillis());
  }
}
```

> *Does the usage of DateTime make this a Sociable*
> *Unit Test? In the Types of Tests chapter I state:*
> *This constraint does not apply to any primitive*
> *or Java class that has a literal (e.g. int, Integer,*
> *String, etc).* I would also extend this exception for
> value objects. In this type of situation I prefer to
> take the most straightforward path: simply use
> the value object.

While these tests do pass, they provide an opportunity for

great frustration in the future.

The first test in `RentalTest` sets the current millis to a fixed point, and never resets to the system clock. Forgetting to reset global state is a common and often costly mistake. Most testing frameworks do not guarantee consistent ordering of test execution, thus it's possible for other tests to pass today and fail in the future due to execution order. Test execution order can often depend on something surprising such as a hashcode. As a result, tests will often begin failing at times when you're working in a completely different portion of the codebase, and for what feels like a completely random reason.

The obvious solution is to always reset the global state, and the test below demonstrates exactly that.

```
public class RentalTest {
  @Test
  public void creationDateTimeNow() {
    DateTimeUtils.setCurrentMillisFixed(1000);
    Rental rental = a.rental.build();
    assertEquals(
      1000,
      rental.getCreationDateTime()
      .getMillis());
    DateTimeUtils.setCurrentMillisSystem();
  }

  @Test
  public void creationDateTimeSet() {
    Rental rental =
      a.rental.w(
        new DateTime(199)).build();
    assertEquals(
      199,
      rental.getCreationDateTime()
      .getMillis());
  }
}
```

The tests above are all passing, and global state is correctly reset; however, when I see tests like the one above, I can't help but grow uncomfortable.

The tests above predictably cause me to complain about the violation of the *Assert Last* principle - though, that's hardly the biggest issue. The largest issue is the opportunity for things to go very wrong before developers are provided any automated feedback.

If the setCurrentMillisSystem call is removed, the test continues passing. Depending on ordering, other tests may continue passing as well... until they don't. At that point you're likely to be far removed from the context that would help determine the cause of the failures.

Unsurprisingly, I prefer a solution that solves this issue on a global scale. The following Solitary class is the same as what was found in the previous subsection, with the addition of setting the current millis to 1000.

```
public class Solitary {
  @Before
  public void setup() {
    FileWriterGateway.disallowAccess = true;
    DateTimeUtils.setCurrentMillisFixed(1000);
  }
}
```

There are many strategies I could have gone with to address my above concern, e.g. @Before or @After each test, call setCurrentMillisSystem. While those solutions would address my concern, I prefer calling setCurrentMillisFixed and providing a constant value that can also be used within the test. As you can see from the following test, providing a constant current millis completely removes the need for DateTimeUtils within RentalTest.

```
public class RentalTest extends Solitary {
  @Test
  public void creationDateTimeNow() {
    Rental rental = a.rental.build();
    assertEquals(
      1000,
      rental.getCreationDateTime()
      .getMillis());
  }

  @Test
  public void creationDateTimeSet() {
    Rental rental =
      a.rental.w(
        new DateTime(199)).build();
    assertEquals(
      199,
      rental.getCreationDateTime()
      .getMillis());
  }
}
```

Complete coverage, concise code, dependence on global constants - those are the kinds of tests I prefer to maintain.

Using Speed To Your Advantage

A test suite improves every time you convert a *Sociable Unit Tests* that cross boundaries to a *Solitary Unit Tests* providing approximately the same ROI. Faster feedback of equal quality is always desired. With that in mind, there's another test suite improvement that I recommend: always run all of the *Solitary Unit Tests* first, and run the *Sociable Unit Tests* if and only if all of the *Solitary Unit Tests* pass. This approach can be abbreviated to *sociable if solitary*.

The *Solitary Unit Tests* will be faster by design, and the short circuiting aspect of *sociable if solitary* allows you to immediately fix broken tests rather than wait for slower test execution to complete.

In Chapter 3 I recommended fixing broken *Solitary Unit Tests* before fixing *Sociable Unit Tests*. *Solitary Unit Tests* generally provide greater defect localization, thus it's logical to start there when looking for the origin of a failure. In addition to the speed benefits, prioritizing *Solitary Unit Test* failures happens naturally when you follow *sociable if solitary*.

Avoiding Cascading Failures With Solitary Unit Tests

I previously stated:

1. *Sociable Unit Tests* are more susceptible to cascading failures
2. Few things kill productivity and motivation faster than cascading test failures.

I stand by those statements, and the following examples will show the evolution of a test suite from brittle to robust. When writing *State Verification* tests you'll have a Class Under Test and 0 or more collaborators. If collaborators are required, you'll be forced to select one of the following.

- use an instance of a concrete class
- use an instance of a hand-rolled stub
- use an instance created by a mocking framework

Using an instance of a concrete class is by far the most common choice, and the starting point for the examples in this section.

The following 11 tests have concrete class collaborators, and are what I would classify as *Sociable Unit Tests.*

```java
public class CustomerTest {
  @Test
  public void noRentalsStatement() {
    assertEquals(
      "Rental record for Jim\nAmount owed " +
      "is 0.0\n" +
      "You earned 0 frequent renter points",
      a.customer.build().statement());
  }

  @Test
  public void oneRentalStatement() {
    assertEquals(
      "Rental record for Jim\n" +
      "\tGodfather 4 9.0\n" +
      "Amount owed is 9.0\n" +
      "You earned 2 frequent renter points",
      a.customer.w(
        a.rental).build().statement());
  }
```

```
@Test
public void twoRentalsStatement() {
  assertEquals(
    "Rental record for Jim\n" +
    "\tGodfather 4 9.0\n" +
    "\tGodfather 4 9.0\n" +
    "Amount owed is 18.0\n" +
    "You earned 4 frequent renter points",
    a.customer.w(
      a.rental, a.rental).build()
    .statement());
}


@Test
public void noRentalsGetTotalPoints() {
  assertEquals(
    0,
    a.customer.build().getTotalPoints());
}


@Test
public void oneRentalGetTotalPoints() {
  assertEquals(
    2,
    a.customer.w(
      a.rental).build().getTotalPoints());
}
```

```
@Test
public void twoRentalsGetTotalPoints() {
  assertEquals(
    4,
    a.customer.w(a.rental, a.rental)
    .build()
    .getTotalPoints());
}

// 3 tests for htmlStatement()
// left to the imagination
}


public class RentalTest {
  @Test
  public void getPointsFromMovie() {
    assertEquals(
      2, a.rental.build().getPoints());
  }
}


public class MovieTest {
  @Test
  public void getPoints() {
    assertEquals(
      2, a.movie.build().getPoints(2));
  }
}
```

I believe these tests are about as well written as possible - for tests that use concrete collaborators. The CustomerTest class focuses exclusively on String building and point summing functionality. The delegation of points per movie is tested in RentalTest. The actual point value is tested in MovieTest. The functionality of the system is well tested, and the tests are focused on testing only the functionality within the Class Under Test.

Unfortunately, all it takes is one character to make you question the value of all of the above tests. The failures you see below were created by a one character change requested by the business.

```
JUnit version 4.11
...E.E.E.E
There were 4 failures:
1) twoRentalsStatement(sociable.CustomerTest)
org.junit.ComparisonFailure: expected:<... is 18.0
You earned [4] frequent renter poi...> but was:<.\
.. is 18.0
You earned [6] frequent renter poi...>
2) oneRentalGetTotalPoints(sociable.CustomerTest)
java.lang.AssertionError: expected:<2> but was:<3>
3) oneRentalStatement(sociable.CustomerTest)
org.junit.ComparisonFailure: expected:<...d is 9.0
You earned [2] frequent renter poi...> but was:<.\
..d is 9.0
You earned [3] frequent renter poi...>
4) twoRentalsGetTotalPoints(sociable.CustomerTest)
java.lang.AssertionError: expected:<4> but was:<6>

FAILURES!!!
Tests run: 6,  Failures: 4
```

note: had I added the 3 htmlStatement tests, 2 of those would be failing as well.

```
JUnit version 4.11
.E
There was 1 failure:
1) getPointsFromMovie(sociable.RentalTest)
java.lang.AssertionError: expected:<2> but was:<3>

FAILURES!!!
Tests run: 1,  Failures: 1
```

```
JUnit version 4.11
.E
There was 1 failure:
1) getPoints(sociable.MovieTest)
java.lang.AssertionError: expected:<2> but was:<3>

FAILURES!!!
Tests run: 1,  Failures: 1
```

The change that would cause 8 of 11 tests to fail can be found below.

```
public class NewReleasePrice extends Price {

  @Override
  public double getCharge(int daysRented) {
    return daysRented * 3;
  }

  @Override
  public int getPoints(int daysRented) {
    if (daysRented > 1)
      return 3; // was 2
    return 1;
  }
}
```

The change the business requested, *New Releases rented for more than 1 day should result in 3 points*, resulted in a failure for every test that was intentionally or unintentionally coupled to the implementation of the NewReleasePrice class.

If your collaborators are instances of concrete classes, you're bound to encounter cascading failures like the example above. I find these failures to be momentum killers. You (correctly) made a simple change requested by the business and your tests immediately transformed from valuable regression protectors to noisy pedants. Within all the failure feedback there is some signal; approximately 3 lines out of 300 are helpful (the actual output contains long stacktraces). It's hard to work effectively when dealing with a 1:100 signal to noise ratio.

I only know of 2 solutions for reducing cascading failures of this type.

- make the tests more intelligent
- make the tests more ignorant

These cascading failures are often avoided by creating complicated tests with intimate knowledge of the collaborators. The original example from Chapter 1 is a great example of tests that will not fail in the way shown above. The original CustomerTest class relies on its knowledge of the methods of both Rental and Movie to avoid cascading failures.

If you're willing to force your teammates to digest the (test helper) code necessary for intelligent tests, you may never feel the pain of cascading failures. However, if you prefer tests that expect literals and follow other patterns I've detailed thus far, you'll need to find a way to dumb the tests down a bit.

Class Under Test

The obvious answer is to replace all collaborators with mocks; therefore converting all of our tests to *Solitary Unit Tests.* Cascading failures are the primary reason I prefer to use the term Class Under Test when I'm defining *Solitary Unit Tests.* Class Under Test reminds you to think in terms of testing the class, **and only the class**, that's under test.

> note: I never verify any of the following *mocks*, thus I (in theory) consider them to be *stubs*, not mocks. However, since I'm calling the mock method, I believe it's less confusing if I refer to the collaborators as mocks. In practice I often define my own stub method (shown later) that does little but delegate and more clearly express my intent.

The following tests are the result of taking the tests above and replacing the collaborators with mocks.

```
public class CustomerTest {
  @Test
  public void noRentalsStatement() {
    assertEquals(
      "Rental record for Jim\nAmount owed " +
      "is 0.0\n" +
      "You earned 0 frequent renter points",
      a.customer.build().statement());
  }

  @Test
  public void oneRentalStatement() {
    Rental rental = mock(Rental.class);
    when(rental.getLineItem())
      .thenReturn("Godfather 4 9.0");
    when(rental.getCharge())
      .thenReturn(9.0);
    when(rental.getPoints())
      .thenReturn(2);
    assertEquals(
      "Rental record for Jim\n" +
      "\tGodfather 4 9.0\n" +
      "Amount owed is 9.0\n" +
      "You earned 2 frequent renter points",
      a.customer.w(rental).build()
      .statement());
  }
```

```
@Test
public void twoRentalsStatement() {
  Rental one = mock(Rental.class);
  when(one.getLineItem())
    .thenReturn("Godfather 4 9.0");
  when(one.getCharge())
    .thenReturn(9.0);
  when(one.getPoints())
    .thenReturn(2);
  Rental two = mock(Rental.class);
  when(two.getLineItem())
    .thenReturn("Godfather 4 9.0");
  when(two.getCharge())
    .thenReturn(9.0);
  when(two.getPoints())
    .thenReturn(2);
  assertEquals(
    "Rental record for Jim\n" +
    "\tGodfather 4 9.0\n" +
    "\tGodfather 4 9.0\n" +
    "Amount owed is 18.0\n" +
    "You earned 4 frequent renter points",
    a.customer.w(one, two).build()
    .statement());
}

@Test
public void noRentalsGetTotalPoints() {
  assertEquals(
    0,
    a.customer.build().getTotalPoints());
}
```

```
@Test
public void oneRentalGetTotalPoints() {
  Rental rental = mock(Rental.class);
  when(rental.getPoints())
    .thenReturn(2);
  assertEquals(
    2,
    a.customer.w(
      rental).build().getTotalPoints());
}

@Test
public void twoRentalsGetTotalPoints() {
  Rental one = mock(Rental.class);
  when(one.getPoints())
    .thenReturn(2);
  Rental two = mock(Rental.class);
  when(two.getPoints())
    .thenReturn(3);
  assertEquals(
    5,
    a.customer.w(
      one, two).build().getTotalPoints());
}
}
```

```java
public class RentalTest {
  @Test
  public void getPointsFromMovie() {
    Movie movie = mock(Movie.class);
    when(movie.getPoints(2))
      .thenReturn(2);
    assertEquals(
      2,
      a.rental.w(
        2).w(movie).build().getPoints());
  }
}
```

When run, the previous examples demonstrate why I believe it's worth the effort to create *Solitary Unit Tests*. The new CustomerTest and RentalTest classes are no longer susceptible to cascading failures due to internal changes to collaborators. Removing the possibility of cascading failures is always a good thing.

Time to celebrate, praise mocks, and move on, right? Not so fast.

The business decided to introduce the idea of a VIP customer. The existing Rental.getPoints method needs to be kept around for other purposes; however, Customer.getTotalPoints now uses a newly introduced Rental.getPoints(boolean vipFlag) overload. The new behavior is added to Movie and Rental and all is well.

```java
public class Rental {

  Movie movie;
  private int daysRented;
  private boolean started;

  public Rental(
    Movie movie, int daysRented) {
    this.movie = movie;
    this.daysRented = daysRented;
  }

  public double getCharge() {
    return movie.getCharge(daysRented);
  }

  public int getPoints() {
    return
      movie.getPoints(daysRented, false);
  }

  public int getPoints(boolean vipFlag) {
    return
      movie.getPoints(daysRented, vipFlag);
  }

  public String getLineItem() {
    return
      movie.getTitle() + " " + getCharge();
  }
}
```

You can now make the final changes to `Customer.getTotalPoints` and run the tests. The output below is what you'll find.

```
JUnit version 4.11
...E.E.E.E
There were 4 failures:
1) twoRentalsStatement(solitary.CustomerTest)
org.junit.ComparisonFailure: expected:<... is 18.0
You earned [4] frequent renter poi...> but was:<.\
.. is 18.0
You earned [0] frequent renter poi...>
2) oneRentalGetTotalPoints(solitary.CustomerTest)
java.lang.AssertionError: expected:<2> but was:<0>
3) oneRentalStatement(solitary.CustomerTest)
org.junit.ComparisonFailure: expected:<...d is 9.0
You earned [2] frequent renter poi...> but was:<.\
..d is 9.0
You earned [0] frequent renter poi...>
4) twoRentalsGetTotalPoints(solitary.CustomerTest)
java.lang.AssertionError: expected:<5> but was:<0>

FAILURES!!!
Tests run: 6,   Failures: 4
```

> (Well, getting that output might actually be pre-
> ferred. You'll actually get that output and 200
> stacktrace lines.)

The root cause of these cascading failures is different, but the result is the same: time wasted updating very loosely related tests, motivation evaporating, and perhaps a bit of faith lost in testing.

Luckily things don't have to be that way. When converting from concrete classes to mocks we were able to keep the expected literals unchanged by specifying return values, but there's no reason the tests need to remain so pedantic.

The tests below show how the statement method can be verified using the default values returned by the Rental mocks. As I said in the *Implementation Overspecification* section, I see no ROI on providing non-default return values when the goal of my test is to verify String building.

With that in mind, I removed the *Implementation Overspecification* in CustomerTest. The result can be seen below.

```java
public class CustomerTest {
  @Test
  public void noRentalsStatement() {
    assertEquals(
      "Rental record for Jim\nAmount owed " +
      "is 0.0\n" +
      "You earned 0 frequent renter points",
      a.customer.build().statement());
  }

  @Test
  public void oneRentalStatement() {
    Rental rental = mock(Rental.class);
    assertEquals(
      "Rental record for Jim\n\tnull\n" +
      "Amount owed is 0.0\n" +
      "You earned 0 frequent renter points",
      a.customer.w(
        rental).build().statement());
  }

  @Test
  public void twoRentalsStatement() {
    Rental rental = mock(Rental.class);
    assertEquals(
      "Rental record for Jim\n\tnull\n" +
      "\tnull\nAmount owed is 0.0\n" +
      "You earned 0 frequent renter points",
      a.customer.w(
        rental, rental).build().statement());
  }
```

```java
@Test
public void noRentalsGetTotalPoints() {
  assertEquals(
    0,
    a.customer.build().getTotalPoints());
}

@Test
public void oneRentalGetTotalPoints() {
  Rental rental = mock(Rental.class);
  when(rental.getPoints())
    .thenReturn(2);
  assertEquals(
    2,
    a.customer.w(
      rental).build().getTotalPoints());
}

@Test
public void twoRentalsGetTotalPoints() {
  Rental one = mock(Rental.class);
  when(one.getPoints())
    .thenReturn(2);
  Rental two = mock(Rental.class);
  when(two.getPoints())
    .thenReturn(3);
  assertEquals(
    5,
    a.customer.w(
      one, two).build().getTotalPoints());
}
}
```

When `Customer.getTotalPoints` is updated to call
`.getPoints(vipFlag)` of `rental` the tests will fail with the
following output.

```
JUnit version 4.11
....E..E
There were 2 failures:
1) oneRentalGetTotalPoints(solitary.CustomerTest)
java.lang.AssertionError: expected:<2> but was:<0>
2) twoRentalsGetTotalPoints(solitary.CustomerTest)
java.lang.AssertionError: expected:<5> but was:<0>

FAILURES!!!
Tests run: 6,  Failures: 2
```

That's the kind of failure that I appreciate. A change was made
to `getTotalPoints` and *only* the tests for `getTotalPoints` are
failing.

We've made our tests even more resilient to cascading failures, and (as I said before) that is always a good thing.

If you didn't see the value in writing *Solitary Unit Tests* while
reading chapter 3, I hope the discussion of Class Under Test
and the example code make clear why I've chosen such strict
guidelines. Likewise, I hope the examples immediately above
clarify why I find it so important to avoid *Implementation
Overspecification.*

Revisiting the Definition of Solitary Unit Test

In the One Assertion Per Test section of Improving Assertions I made the following statement:

> At this point you may wonder if the collaboration between `Movie` and `ChildrensPrice` forces `MovieTest` to be classified as a *Sociable Unit Test*.

The code in question can be found below.

```
public class MovieTest {
  @Test
  public void getChargeForChildrens() {
    assertEquals(
      1.5,
      a.movie.w(
        CHILDREN).build().getCharge(1),
      0);
    assertEquals(
      1.5,
      a.movie.w(
        CHILDREN).build().getCharge(2),
      0);
    assertEquals(
      1.5,
      a.movie.w(
        CHILDREN).build().getCharge(3),
      0);
    assertEquals(
      3.0,
      a.movie.w(
        CHILDREN).build().getCharge(4),
      0);
    assertEquals(
      4.5,
      a.movie.w(
        CHILDREN).build().getCharge(5),
      0);
  }
}
```

```java
public class Movie {

  public enum Type {
    REGULAR, NEW_RELEASE, CHILDREN, UNKNOWN;
  }

  private String title;
  Price price;

  public Movie(
    String title, Movie.Type priceCode) {
    this.title = title;
    setPriceCode(priceCode);
  }

  public String getTitle() {
    return title;
  }
```

```
  private void setPriceCode(
    Movie.Type priceCode) {
    switch (priceCode) {
    case CHILDREN:
      price = new ChildrensPrice();
      break;
    case NEW_RELEASE:
      price = new NewReleasePrice();
      break;
    case REGULAR:
      price = new RegularPrice();
      break;
    default:
      throw new IllegalArgumentException(
        "invalid price code");
    }
  }

  public double getCharge(int daysRented) {
    return price.getCharge(daysRented);
  }

  public int getPoints(int daysRented) {
    return price.getPoints(daysRented);
  }
}
```

```
public class ChildrensPrice extends Price {

  @Override
  public double getCharge(int daysRented) {
    double amount = 1.5;
    if (daysRented > 2) // *was 3*
      amount += (daysRented - 2) * 1.5;
    return amount;
  }
}
```

Technically the constraint is:

> The *Class Under Test* should be the only concrete
> class found in a test.

Since ChildrensPrice isn't found within the test, the constraint has been satisfied, technically. Honestly though, the point of the constraints are to make your life easier, not to provide you with dogma to blindly follow.

Every piece of advice that I've given should be taken as: *You should do X, unless it hurts.* Blindly following advice will only get you into trouble, and turn a positive ROI activity into a potentially negative ROI burden.

In the above example the Movie instances will collaborate with instances of ChildrensPrice. ChildrensPrice is a very straightforward class that's easy to collaborate with. It doesn't hurt, so the pragmatic thing to do is leave the domain code as is and deal with the concrete collaboration.

Conversely, if the collaboration with ChildrensPrice were causing pain (such as cascading failures) you could inject a `PriceFactory` that was responsible for creating the `Price` subclasses. The addition of a `PriceFactory` would allow you to create stub `Price` instances in the `MovieTest`. This entire pattern is tried and true; however, it's not free. I wouldn't hesitate to introduce it if it cleaned up some painful tests. Likewise, I wouldn't dare introduce it unless it cleaned up some painful tests. All code must be maintained; there's no point in adding more unless it improves the situation.

As I mentioned at the beginning of the book, blindly following constraints isn't a good idea. However, understanding and doing everything you can to follow proven advice while balancing the needs of your context will always be the right choice.

Questionable Tests

There are several types of tests that I simply don't write. I find the following test types to provide negative ROI more often than not. This is not to say that they *cannot* provide positive ROI. I'm merely suggesting that it's often worth your time to closely evaluate the ROI of tests of the following types.

Testing Language Features or Standard Library Classes

Every now and then I run into someone testing a language feature or a class from the standard library of whatever language they're using. The vast majority of the time, I can't think of a logical reason to do such a thing and I recommend deleting the test. Below you'll find examples of what I traditionally find to be negative ROI tests.

```java
public class JavaTest {
  @Test
  public void arrayListGet() {
    ArrayList<Integer> list =
      new ArrayList<Integer>();
    list.add(1);
    assertEquals(
      Integer.valueOf(1), list.get(0));
  }

  @Test
  public void hashMapGet() {
    HashMap<Integer, String> map =
      new HashMap<Integer, String>();
    map.put(1, "a str");
    assertEquals("a str", map.get(1));
  }

  @Test
  public void throwCatch() {
    Exception ex = null;
    try {
      throw new RuntimeException("ex");
    } catch (Exception eCaught) {
      ex = eCaught;
    }
    assertEquals("ex", ex.getMessage());
  }
}
```

Whether or not these tests provide ROI comes down to whether or not you trust your language and/or standard library.

In the spirit of full disclosure, I once worked on a team that wanted to run on bleeding edge versions of their language. That team used these tests to give them confidence that an upgrade would not break their application. As usual, consider your context when determining ROI.

Testing Framework Features or Classes

Take all of the above commentary and apply it to framework features and classes as well. Below is a reasonable test for Joda, but is it really necessary?

```java
public class JodaTest {
  @Test
  public void parseStr() {
    assertEquals(
      286347600000L,
      DateTime.parse(
        "1979-01-28").getMillis());
  }
}
```

Similarly to what was said in the previous subsection: These tests might make sense if you're often upgrading a framework and don't trust it. If you're not upgrading or you do trust the framework, it's worth looking at the ROI of these tests and likely deleting them.

Testing Private Methods

The question of whether or not to test private methods has been around as long as people have been testing. I wouldn't claim that the answer is *absolutely not*, but I've rarely seen it as a positive ROI activity. If a private method is important enough to test, you likely have a tested public method that relies on that private method. If you're already testing the public method that's coupled to the private method, there's often little value in providing the additional test for the private method.

At times you may find a private method complicated enough that it feels like a test might be in order. In that situation I like to take a step back and determine if the tests are pushing me towards a better object model. In the examples we've previously seen, the entire Price class could probably have been managed via private methods in Movie; however, I would argue the current object model is both easier to test as well as maintain.

Custom Assertions

Another option that often improves a test suite is the creation of custom assertions. Custom assertions can take *assert* structural duplication and replace it with a concise, globally useful single assertion.

> Structural Duplication: The overall pattern of the code is the same, but the details differ.

We've already touched on custom assertions previously in the *Assert Last* section. The following Assert class contains the assertThrows method we previously used to verify an exception was thrown.

```
public class Assert {
  public static void assertThrows(
    Class ex, Runnable runnable) {
    Exception exThrown = null;
    try {
      runnable.run();
    } catch (Exception exThrownActual) {
      exThrown = exThrownActual;
    }
    if (null == exThrown)
      fail("No exception thrown");
    else
      assertEquals(ex, exThrown.getClass());
  }
}
```

Custom assertions provide at least two advantages to structural duplication.

- A higher level concept can be consistently tested.
- Custom assertions can be tested, removing mistakes that are common with copy/paste of structural duplication.

Below you'll find two versions of the same test - creating a Movie of an UNKNOWN type should throw an IllegalArgumentException.

```
public class MovieTest {
  @Test
  public void invalidTitleCustomAssertion() {
    assertThrows(
      IllegalArgumentException.class,
      () -> a.movie.w(UNKNOWN).build());
  }

  @Test
  public void invalidTitleWithoutCA() {
    Exception e = null;
    try {
      a.movie.w(UNKNOWN).build();
    } catch (Exception ex) {
      e = ex;
    }
    assertEquals(
      IllegalArgumentException.class,
      e.getClass());
  }
}
```

I couldn't resist using a lambda to emphasize the superiority of solving this problem with a custom assertion. The lambda version is beautifully concise, and it also ensures developers aren't bitten by the try/missing-fail/catch bug I described in the *Assert Last* section.

In addition, we can write tests for assertThrows. If assertThrows is well tested and invalidTitleCustomAssertion fails, you'll feel confident that the problem is very likely in your domain code. Conversely, If invalidTitleWithoutCA fails, who knows if the problem is in the domain code or an issue with the test itself.

With that in mind, I'd create the following tests to ensure assertThrows works as expected.

```java
public class AssertTest {
  @Test
  public void failIfNoThrow() {
    AssertionError e = null;
    try {
      assertThrows(
        IllegalArgumentException.class,
        mock(Runnable.class));
    } catch (AssertionError ex) {
      e = ex;
    }
    assertEquals(
      AssertionError.class,
      e.getClass());
  }

  @Test
  public void failWithMessageIfNoThrow() {
    AssertionError e = null;
    try {
      assertThrows(
        IllegalArgumentException.class,
        mock(Runnable.class));
    } catch (AssertionError ex) {
      e = ex;
    }
    assertEquals(
      "No exception thrown",
      e.getMessage());
  }
```

```
@Test
public void failIfClassMismatch() {
  AssertionError e = null;
  try {
    assertThrows(
      IllegalArgumentException.class,
      () -> {
        throw new RuntimeException("");});
  } catch (AssertionError ex) {
    e = ex;
  }
  assertEquals(
    AssertionError.class,
    e.getClass());
}
```

```
@Test
public void failWithMessageIfClassWrong() {
  AssertionError e = null;
  try {
    assertThrows(
      IllegalArgumentException.class,
      () -> {
        throw new RuntimeException("");});
  } catch (AssertionError ex) {
    e = ex;
  }
  assertEquals(
    "expected:<class java.lang."+
    "IllegalArgumentException> "+
    "but was:<class java.lang."+
    "RuntimeException>",
    e.getMessage());
}
```

```java
@Test
public void passWithCorrectException() {
  AssertionError e = null;
  try {
    assertThrows(
      RuntimeException.class,
      () -> {
        throw new RuntimeException("");}});
  } catch (AssertionError ex) {
    e = ex;
  }
  assertEquals(null, e);
  }
}
```

Not the prettiest tests you've ever seen; however, they surely give you the confidence you need to use assertThrows to create beautiful tests everywhere else an *expected exception* test is required.

Custom Assertions on Value Objects

In the *Expect Literals* section of Chapter 4 I created the following example test.

```java
public class MovieTest {
  @Test
  public void compareDates() {
    Movie godfather =
      a.movie.w(
        new Date(70261200000L)).build();
    assertEquals(
      "1972-03-24",
      new SimpleDateFormat(
        "yyyy-MM-dd").format(
          godfather.releaseDate())));
  }
}
```

That test is what I would consider *fine*. It's not great, but it's not ugly enough that I'd bother doing anything else - if it were the only test in the codebase of that shape. That said, if there were several assertions that focused on the date, I would probably create the following custom assertion.

```
public class Assert {
  public static void assertDateWithFormat(
    String expected,
    String format,
    Date dt) {
    assertEquals(
      expected,
      new SimpleDateFormat(
        format).format(dt));
  }
}
```

The assertDateWithFormat method is very simple, and it allows me to create the simplified version of MovieTest shown below.

```
public class MovieTest {
  @Test
  public void compareDates() {
    Movie godfather =
      a.movie.w(
        new Date(70261200000L)).build();
    assertDateWithFormat(
      "1972-03-24",
      "yyyy-MM-dd",
      godfather.releaseDate());
  }
}
```

The difference between the previous individual test and the version from *Expect Literals* isn't drastic; however, the more assertDateWithFormat is used the more you'll appreciate its existence.

Custom Assertions for Money

It wouldn't take very long for our current object model to give us floating point rounding errors, forcing us to add a `Money` value object to the system. Since this book is about testing, not *designing the best Money class ever*, I'm going to use the following contrived implementation (it's little more than a wrapper on `BigDecimal`).

```java
public class Money {
  private BigDecimal val;

  public Money(double val) {
    this(BigDecimal.valueOf(val));
  }

  public Money(BigDecimal val) {
    this.val = val;
  }

  public Money add(double d) {
    return new Money(
      val.add(BigDecimal.valueOf(d)));
  }

  public Money add(Money m) {
    return new Money(val.add(m.val));
  }

  public double toDouble() {
    return val
      .setScale(2, BigDecimal.ROUND_HALF_UP)
      .doubleValue();
  }
}
```

The above Money class is easily tested, as shown below.

```
public class MoneyTest {
  @Test
  public void doubleAddition() {
    assertEquals(
      11.0,
      a.money.w(1.0).build().add(
        10.0).toDouble(),
      0);
  }

  @Test
  public void moneyAddition() {
    assertEquals(
      11.0,
      a.money.w(1.0).build().add(
        a.money.w(10.0).build()).toDouble(),
      0);
  }

  @Test
  public void oneDecimalToDouble() {
    assertEquals(
      1.0,
      a.money.w(1.0).build().toDouble(),
      0);
  }
```

```
@Test
public void twoDecimalToDouble() {
  assertEquals(
    1.12,
    a.money.w(1.12).build().toDouble(),
    0);
}


@Test
public void thrDecimalUpToDouble() {
  assertEquals(
    1.12,
    a.money.w(1.123).build().toDouble(),
    0);
}


@Test
public void thrDecimalDownToDouble() {
  assertEquals(
    1.13,
    a.money.w(1.125).build().toDouble(),
    0);
  }
}
```

The introduction of Money will be fairly pervasive in our object model. Below you can find the updated Movie class, which now returns a Money from getCharge.

```
public class Movie {

  public enum Type {
    REGULAR, NEW_RELEASE, CHILDREN;
  }

  private String title;
  Price price;

  public Movie(
    String title, Movie.Type priceCode) {
    this.title = title;
    setPriceCode(priceCode);
  }

  private void setPriceCode(
    Movie.Type priceCode) {
    switch (priceCode) {
    case CHILDREN:
      price = new ChildrensPrice();
      break;
    case NEW_RELEASE:
      price = new NewReleasePrice();
      break;
    case REGULAR:
      price = new RegularPrice();
      break;
    }
  }
```

```
public Money getCharge(int daysRented) {
  return price.getCharge(daysRented);
  }
}
```

The MovieTest class below is similar to what we previously saw in One Assertion Per Test, modified to call toDouble on the Money instance returned from getCharge.

```java
public class MovieTest {
  @Test
  public void getChargeForChildrens1Day() {
    assertEquals(
      1.5,
      a.movie.w(
        CHILDREN).build().getCharge(
          1).toDouble(),
      0);
  }

  @Test
  public void getChargeForChildrens2Day() {
    assertEquals(
      1.5,
      a.movie.w(
        CHILDREN).build().getCharge(
          2).toDouble(),
      0);
  }

  @Test
  public void getChargeForChildrens3Day() {
    assertEquals(
      1.5,
      a.movie.w(
        CHILDREN).build().getCharge(
          3).toDouble(),
      0);
  }
```

```
@Test
public void getChargeForChildrens4Day() {
  assertEquals(
    3.0,
    a.movie.w(
      CHILDREN).build().getCharge(
        4).toDouble(),
    0);
}

@Test
public void getChargeForChildrens5Day() {
  assertEquals(
    4.5,
    a.movie.w(
      CHILDREN).build().getCharge(
        5).toDouble(),
    0);
}
}
```

All of the tests shown thus far in this subsection are *fine* (as previously defined). That said, the duplication that's beginning to appear is pointing me towards a custom assertion.

Several of the tests we've seen for Money and Movie contain the following structural duplication.

```
assertEquals(
  doubleLiteral,
  getSomeMoney().toDouble(),
  0)
```

Structural duplication within a single test case doesn't warrant creating a custom assertion - the duplication isn't global enough to justify a global solution. However, now that we've seen structural duplication in Money and Movie it's probably time to create an assertMoney. The fact that we know we're going to see the same duplication in Rental and Customer makes a custom assertion an obvious choice.

The following assertMoney method can both be used to clean up our existing tests as well as be independently tested similarly to (the previously shown) assertThrows.

```
public class Assert {
  public static void assertMoney(
    double d, Money m) {
    assertEquals(d, m.toDouble(), 0);
  }
}
```

> note: If you prefer a more descriptive name such as assertMoneyToDouble, go for it. The descriptiveness of the name has no effect on whether or not to use a custom assertion.

With assertMoney available, the MoneyTest class cleans up nicely.

```
public class MoneyTest {
  @Test
  public void doubleAddition() {
    assertMoney(
      11.0, a.money.w(1.0).build().add(10.0));
  }

  @Test
  public void moneyAddition() {
    assertMoney(
      11.0,
      a.money.w(1.0).build().add(
        a.money.w(10.0).build()));
  }

  @Test
  public void oneDecimalToDouble() {
    assertMoney(
      1.0, a.money.w(1.0).build());
  }

  @Test
  public void twoDecimalToDouble() {
    assertMoney(
      1.12, a.money.w(1.12).build());
  }

  @Test
  public void thrDecimalUpToDouble() {
    assertMoney(
      1.12, a.money.w(1.123).build());
  }
```

```
@Test
public void thrDecimalDownToDouble() {
  assertMoney(
    1.13, a.money.w(1.125).build());
  }
}
```

Likewise, the MovieTest structural duplication can be easily removed, resulting in concise and maintainable tests.

```java
public class MovieTest {
  @Test
  public void getChargeForChildrens1Day() {
    assertMoney(
      1.5,
      a.movie.w(
        CHILDREN).build().getCharge(1));
  }

  @Test
  public void getChargeForChildrens2Day() {
    assertMoney(
      1.5,
      a.movie.w(
        CHILDREN).build().getCharge(2));
  }

  @Test
  public void getChargeForChildrens3Day() {
    assertMoney(
      1.5,
      a.movie.w(
        CHILDREN).build().getCharge(3));
  }

  @Test
  public void getChargeForChildrens4Day() {
    assertMoney(
      3.0,
      a.movie.w(
        CHILDREN).build().getCharge(4));
  }
```

```
@Test
public void getChargeForChildrens5Day() {
  assertMoney(
    4.5,
    a.movie.w(
      CHILDREN).build().getCharge(5));
  }
}
```

The change to Rental and RentalTest is obvious, and easier
to implement with assertMoney in place.

```
public class Rental {

  Movie movie;
  private int daysRented;

  public Rental(
    Movie movie, int daysRented) {
    this.movie = movie;
    this.daysRented = daysRented;
  }

  public Money getCharge() {
    return movie.getCharge(daysRented);
  }
}
```

```
public class RentalTest {
  @Test
  public void getChargeFromMovie() {
    Movie movie = mock(Movie.class);
    when(movie.getCharge(any(Integer.class)))
      .thenReturn(a.money.w(1.5).build());
    assertMoney(
      1.5,
      a.rental.w(movie).build().getCharge());
  }
}
```

A final change to the Customer and CustomerTest classes
complete the addition of Money to our object model, and
further demonstrate the value of our custom assertion.

```
public class Customer {

  private List<Rental> rentals =
    new ArrayList<Rental>();

  public void addRental(Rental rental) {
    rentals.add(rental);
  }

  public Money getTotalCharge() {
    Money total = new Money(0.0);
    for (Rental rental : rentals)
      total = total.add(rental.getCharge());
    return total;
  }
}
```

```java
public class CustomerTest {
  @Test
  public void chargeForNoRentals() {
    assertMoney(
      0.0,
      a.customer.build().getTotalCharge());
  }

  @Test
  public void chargeForOneRental() {
    Rental rental = mock(Rental.class);
    when(rental.getCharge())
      .thenReturn(a.money.w(2.0).build());
    assertMoney(
      2.0,
      a.customer.w(
        rental).build().getTotalCharge());
  }
```

```
@Test
public void chargeForTwoRentals() {
  Rental rental1 = mock(Rental.class);
  when(rental1.getCharge())
    .thenReturn(a.money.w(2.2).build());
  Rental rental2 = mock(Rental.class);
  when(rental2.getCharge())
    .thenReturn(a.money.w(3.5).build());
  assertMoney(
    5.7,
    a.customer.w(
      rental1,
      rental2).build().getTotalCharge());
}
}
```

Global Definition

Custom Assertions can improve a test suite, and they aren't the only example of globally useful code. This section shows how to effectively and concisely create both domain objects and simple stubs. While the examples are concrete, the idea is more abstract: *If you find yourself repeating the same idea in* **multiple test cases**, *look for a higher level concept that can be extracted and reused.*

The abstract idea in this chapter can be valuable; however, remember not to DRY your code with a blowtorch. Duplication, structural or character, within a single test case does not warrant extraction. Instead, look to address duplication within a single test case in the object model itself. Extracting duplication of any type from an individual test case and creating a *"global"* solution is highly likely to create negative ROI.

Creating Domain Objects Within Tests

Sociable Unit Tests consist of a Class Under Test (CUT), and may also involve collaborators. The CUT and collaborators need to be created somewhere. At this point, developers still cannot seem to agree on whether instances should be created using new (vanilla construction), Test Data Builders, Object Mother, or a competing solution.

The examples within this book leave no question as to which solution I prefer; however, I suspect it's worth spending a few paragraphs discussing my preference.

New Is The New New

There's been a recent movement away from containers and towards simply creating your objects with new. This movement has a simple catch-phrase:

> New is the new new.

I first heard the phrase from Joe Walnes; though I've seen Dan North credited as well. The merits of abandoning containers is outside the scope of this book; however, I will quickly mention that I do agree with this movement in general - when we're talking about creating objects within our domain model. My support of new does not extend to tests.

I become deeply disappointed whenever it takes X minutes to implement a feature, and more than 2X minutes to update the test suite. Tests are supposed to make us more effective; how could we ever claim to be effective if we spend more than 66% of our time working on code that will never run in production?

A change that creates cascading failures will likely lead us to the disappointing time ratio described above, thus the previous subsection on how to avoid cascading failures. Unfortunately, using new can quickly put us in the same unenviable position.

Most codebases will instantiate significantly more objects in tests than within a domain model. As an example, in the *Custom Assertions for Money* sample code we created a Money instance four times within the object model and twelve times within the tests.

If we need to add a constructor argument to Money and we create the instances used within the tests using new, we likely spend three times as much time updating the tests as we do updating the object model. Disappointing.

Object Mother

> When you write tests in a reasonably sized sys-
> tem, you find you have to create a lot of example
> data. If I want to test a sick pay calculation on an
> employee, I need an employee. But this isn't just
> a simple object - I'll need the employee's marital
> status, number of dependents, some employment
> and payroll history. Potentially this can be a lot
> of objects to create. This set data is generally
> referred to as the test fixture.

> The first move is to create fixture in the setup
> method of an xunit test - that way it can be reused
> in multiple tests. But the trouble with this is often
> you need similar data in multiple test classes.
> At this point it makes sense to have a factory
> object that can return standard fixtures. –Martin
> Fowler, ObjectMother[19]

In the same write-up Martin is very clear about the potential issues with Object Mother.

By now I suspect it's crystal clear how I feel about code written with a specific subset of tests in mind. In practice I find, as the project progresses, the coupling between the tests and the mothers eventually results in immutable tests. At some point you'll find yourself in need of an instance

---

[19]http://martinfowler.com/bliki/ObjectMother.html

similar to what's already available; unfortunately, you'll be unable to use it without a *"small"* change - a change that causes *"unrelated"* tests to fail as well. At that point you begin digging deeply into the fixture code, and quickly end up in the same disappointing time spent ratio as above.

If you couple your tests, even coupling at the data level, eventually the tests will likely transition from positive to negative ROI.

Test Data Builders

I find Test Data Builders to be a superior option. The guidelines for creating a Test Data Builder are found below.

> For each class you want to use in a test, create a Builder for that class that:
>
> - Has an instance variable for each constructor parameter
> - Initializes its instance variables to commonly used or safe values
> - Has a `build` method that creates a new object using the values in its instance variables
> - Has "chainable" public methods for overriding the values in its instance variables.
>
> –Nat Pryce, Test Data Builders[20]

Creating a test fixture can be both tedious and error prone.

---

[20]http://www.natpryce.com/articles/000714.html

The concerns in *New Is The New New* describe my largest issue with using new to create a test fixture. In stark contrast, if you add a constructor argument to Money and the tests are written as they are in *Custom Assertions for Money*, the same four calls to new in the object model must be updated and the single call to new in the Test Data Builder must be updated.

Using the Test Data Builder pattern we've changed the test:object-model maintenance ratio from 3:1 (using new) to 1:4. While I would classify spending 75% of our time within the tests as *disappointing*, I would gladly classify spending 20% of our time as *working effectively*.

Object Mother is a competing solution that addresses test fixture creation pain; however, it (as Nat points out) does not cope well with *variation in the test data*. Any non-trivial Object Mother is likely to become bloated with duplication and offer no obvious improvement path.

Data Builders provide you the benefits of creating an object with sensible defaults, and provide methods for adding your test specific data - thus keeping your tests decoupled.

Test Data Builder Syntax

An example found on Nat's blog shows the following:

```
anOrder().from(
  aCustomer().with(...)).build();
```

The Test Data Builders found within this book would have the following syntax for the same domain objects.

```
a.order.w(a.customer.w(...)).build();
```

There's at least one other alternative that I could justify using based on context:

```
build(
  order.w(
    customer.w(...)));
```

Nat explains his choice on his blog: *de-emphasize the builders further by instantiating them in clearly named factory methods*[21]

My choice to use a.domainObject is based on the desire to use IntelliSense without having to static import the factory methods. The cost of this choice is maintaining the a class.

Finally, it would be trivial to create a TestDataBuilder interface that defines build, thus enabling the last shown example. The advantage of this solution is the ability to indent the code as shown above.

All three of the above solutions have minor positive and negative aspects. I wouldn't spend too much time worrying about conflicting syntax in Test Data Builder examples. The Test Data Builder pattern is what's truly valuable; the syntax is an implementation detail that doesn't significantly impact ROI.

It's not necessary to pick the perfect syntax on your first attempt at introducing Test Data Builders. Switching from one syntax to another is a bit tedious, but it's not very error prone. You may even find that there's an alternative solution

---

[21]http://www.natpryce.com/articles/000727.html

that's more suited to your context. My advice is to pick one that seems most appealing to your team and incrementally improve where necessary.

Test Data Builder Guidelines Revisited

There's no explicit guideline that states that a builder shouldn't contain an instance variable for non-constructor values; however, I often find that a complex builder is only necessary when working with an overly complicated object model. Furthermore, creating complex builders can quickly lead us to pain similar to what we find when we're using an Object Mother.

As an example, the `CustomerBuilder` currently contains `rentals` that are added after a `Customer` instance has been constructed. Thus far this hasn't been a problem, but there's really no reason to start introducing potentially problematic behavior.

Below you'll find the a class that contains the `CustomerBuilder` (among other things) and one of the `CustomerTest` methods that was found in the *Custom Assertions for Money* section.

```
public class a {
  public static CustomerBuilder customer =
    new CustomerBuilder();
  public static MoneyBuilder money =
    new MoneyBuilder();

  public static class CustomerBuilder {
    Rental[] rentals;

    CustomerBuilder() {
      this(new Rental[0]);
    }

    CustomerBuilder(Rental[] rentals) {
      this.rentals = rentals;
    }

    public CustomerBuilder w(
      Rental... rentals) {
      return new CustomerBuilder(rentals);
    }

    public Customer build() {
      Customer result = new Customer();
      for (Rental rental : rentals) {
        result.addRental(rental);
      }
      return result;
    }
  }
}
```

```java
public static class MoneyBuilder {
  final double val;

  MoneyBuilder() {
    this(1.0);
  }

  MoneyBuilder(double val) {
    this.val = val;
  }

  public MoneyBuilder w(double val) {
    return new MoneyBuilder(val);
  }

  public Money build() {
    return new Money(val);
  }
}
}
```

```
public class CustomerTest {
  @Test
  public void chargeForTwoRentals() {
    Rental rental1 = mock(Rental.class);
    when(rental1.getCharge())
      .thenReturn(a.money.w(2.2).build());
    Rental rental2 = mock(Rental.class);
    when(rental2.getCharge())
      .thenReturn(a.money.w(3.5).build());
    assertMoney(
      5.7,
      a.customer.w(
        rental1,
        rental2).build().getTotalCharge());
  }
}
```

Based on my opinion above, we'll need to remove all references to rentals within the CustomerBuilder inner class.

Following this change, the CustomerTest will need to become to what you see below.

```
public class CustomerTest {
  @Test
  public void chargeForTwoRentals() {
    Rental rental1 = mock(Rental.class);
    when(rental1.getCharge())
      .thenReturn(a.money.w(2.2).build());
    Rental rental2 = mock(Rental.class);
    when(rental2.getCharge())
      .thenReturn(a.money.w(3.5).build());
    Customer customer = a.customer.build();
    customer.addRental(rental1);
    customer.addRental(rental2);
    assertMoney(
      5.7, customer.getTotalCharge());
  }
}
```

This test could be *fine* as is; however, we originally wrote the w(Rental... rentals) method to reduce duplication, and that desire still exists.

Throughout this book I've made claims that duplication within an individual test case can often be removed by making a change to the object model. The code evolution within this subsection serves as a concrete example of that advice put in action.

Specifically, I can improve the tests by applying the following two quick changes to the domain model.

The current Customer class can be found below.

```
public class Customer {
  private List<Rental> rentals =
    new ArrayList<Rental>();

  public void addRental(Rental rental) {
    rentals.add(rental);
  }

  public Money getTotalCharge() {
    Money total = new Money(0.0);
    for (Rental rental : rentals)
      total = total.add(rental.getCharge());
    return total;
  }
}
```

If we change addRental to addRentals and change it to return this, the Customer class would look like the following.

```java
public class Customer {
  private ArrayList<Rental> rentals =
    new ArrayList<Rental>();

  public Customer addRentals(
    Rental... newRentals) {
    rentals.addAll(Arrays.asList(newRentals));
    return this;
  }

  public Money getTotalCharge() {
    Money total = new Money(0.0);
    for (Rental rental : rentals)
      total = total.add(rental.getCharge());
    return total;
  }
}
```

With those changes in place the same method of CustomerTest can be written as what's shown below.

```
public class CustomerTest {
  @Test
  public void chargeForTwoRentals() {
    Rental rental1 = mock(Rental.class);
    when(rental1.getCharge())
      .thenReturn(a.money.w(2.2).build());
    Rental rental2 = mock(Rental.class);
    when(rental2.getCharge())
      .thenReturn(a.money.w(3.5).build());
    assertMoney(
      5.7,
      a.customer.build().addRentals(
        rental1, rental2).getTotalCharge());
  }
}
```

The above test could also be written to declare a Customer local; however, I prefer to eliminate locals whenever possible. This preference is based on the conceptual overhead introduced by locals. Conversely, when an instance is used strictly as an argument, you never need to scan the rest of the test looking for additional usages.

Creating Stubs

It's very common to find collaborators within unit tests, thus it makes sense to evaluate eliminating structural or character duplication specific to stubbing.

Create, Stub, Return

The usage pattern of the stubs from the last `CustomerTest` shown is common enough that I prefer to encapsulate it within a higher level concept. Specifically, I like to capture the following steps with a few methods that can be combined to produce the same result.

1. Create a stub.
2. Stub the result of a single method call.
3. Pass the stub to another method.

As I mentioned at the end of the *Test Data Builders* subsection, I prefer to eliminate locals when possible. The methods provided by Mockito offer no way to create a stub, mock a single method call, and return the mock; however, it's not very complicated to write those methods ourselves.

```java
public class MockitoExtensions {
  @SuppressWarnings("unchecked")
  public static <T> T create(
    Object methodCall) {
    when(methodCall)
      .thenReturn(
        StubBuilder.current.returnValue);
    return (T)
      StubBuilder.current.mockInstance;
  }
  public static <T> StubBuilder<T> stub(
    Class<T> klass) {
    return new StubBuilder<T>(mock(klass));
  }
  public static class StubBuilder<T> {
    public static StubBuilder current;
    public final T mockInstance;
    private Object returnValue;
    public StubBuilder(T mockInstance) {
      current = this;
      this.mockInstance = mockInstance;
    }
    public T from() {
      return mockInstance;
    }
    public StubBuilder<T> returning(
      Object returnValue) {
      this.returnValue = returnValue;
      return this;
    }
  }
}
```

Okay, perhaps it's mildly complicated. Still, with the methods above in place, we're able to remove all the local variables from the last shown CustomerTest class.

```
public class CustomerTest {
  @Test
  public void chargeForTwoRentals() {
    assertMoney(
      5.7,
      a.customer.build().addRentals(
        create(
          stub(Rental.class)
          .returning(a.money.w(2.2).build())
          .from().getCharge()),
        create(
          stub(Rental.class)
          .returning(a.money.w(3.5).build())
          .from().getCharge()))
      .getTotalCharge());
  }
}
```

I believe tests such as the above CustomerTest are some of the most effective tests you could possibly write.

Assume the test is currently failing and you're unfamiliar with Customer and CustomerTest.

- The assertion follows the Assert Last principle, thus you know where to look for the origin of the failure.
- There are no locals, thus there's no need to scan the test for usages.

- The assertion is globally used, thus it's unlikely that navigation will be a prerequisite to understanding.
- The expected value is a literal, thus no navigation is required for understanding.
- The domain object is built using a builder, thus it's unlikely that navigation will be a prerequisite to understanding.
- The domain method `addRentals` is called, which will require navigation prior to understanding
  - This is your first true investment in understanding this test.
- The collaborators are created using general stubbing methods, thus it's unlikely that navigation will be a prerequisite to understanding.
- The return value of the stubbed method is created using a builder, thus it's unlikely that navigation will be a prerequisite to understanding.
- All collaborators are stubs, thus the problem cannot exist in their implementation, more navigation avoided.
- The domain method `getTotalCharge` creates *actual* value; navigation will be required.
  - This is the second and final investment you'll be required to make to understand this test.

It's likely that no test specific code will need to be read to fully understand the test;

In summary, the entire test can largely be understood without any navigation, and as written it's easy to pick out which domain methods will need to be examined to find the source of the failure.

Create, Lambda, Return

The previous MockitoExtensions class uses static state. I suspect some of you were offended by that choice. I created this section as an offer of amends. The following MockitoExtensions implementation allows you to easily create a stub with declared behavior and no local.

```java
public class MockitoExtensions {
  public static <T> T stub(
    Class<T> klass,
    Function<T,Object> f,
    Object returnVal) {
    try {
      T result = mock(klass);
      when(f.apply(result))
        .thenReturn(returnVal);
      return result;
    } catch (Exception e) {
      throw new RuntimeException(e);
    }
  }
}
```

Armed with that implementation of stub the CustomerTest class can be written as follows.

```
public class CustomerTest {
  @Test
  public void chargeForTwoRentals() {
    assertMoney(
      5.7,
      a.customer.build().addRentals(
        stub(Rental.class,
             s -> s.getCharge(),
             a.money.w(2.2).build()),
        stub(Rental.class,
             s -> s.getCharge(),
             a.money.w(3.5).build()))
      .getTotalCharge());
  }
}
```

More Than Creation

With Test Data Builders and the above Mockito Extensions in place, you should be able to concisely create any instances required in your unit tests. Defining globally useful functions for creation is a great start, but there's no need to stop there.

> remember: If you find yourself repeating any idea in **multiple** test cases, (then and only then) look for a higher level concept that can be extracted and reused.

Closing Thoughts

Broad Stack Tests

I previously defined *Solitary Unit Test* strictly and *Sociable Unit Test* as everything else. These definitions work for describing unit tests, but it's unlikely that you'll want to work with unit tests exclusively. In practice there's often another, higher level type of test: Broad Stack Test[22]. Most teams have Broad Stack Tests in what they call Functional Tests, Integration Tests, End-to-End Tests, Smoke Tests, or something similar. These tests are designed to exercise as much of the application as possible, often using an automated tool to drive a UI or deliver out of process messages.

I'm a fan of Broad Stack Tests; however, back in 2009 I decided on what I considered to be a good guideline for Broad Stack Testing:

> Never write more than a dozen Broad Stack Tests.

Broad Stack Tests are almost always complicated and extremely fragile. It's not uncommon for a single change to break an entire suite of Broad Stack Tests. Truthfully, anything related to Broad Stack Testing always comes with an implicit "here be dragons".

I've been responsible for my fair share of Broad Stack Test creation. Despite my best efforts, I've never found a way to write Broad Stack Tests that weren't dominated by complex and implicit logic. Unfortunately, tests with those characteristics often equal heartbreak for teammates that are less familiar with the Broad Stack Tests. Broad Stack Test issues often arise

---

[22]http://martinfowler.com/bliki/BroadStackTest.html

from concurrency, stubbing external resources, configuration properties, internal state exposure and manipulation, 3rd party components, and everything else that is required to test your application under production-like circumstances.

To make things worse, these tests are often your last line of defense. Most issues that these tests would catch are caught by a unit test that is better designed to pinpoint where the issue originates. Finally, and worst of all, nine out of ten times the tests report failure it's due to the test infrastructure (not an actual flaw in the application) and it takes a significant amount of time to figure out how to fix the infrastructure (with no actual benefit to the domain model).

I've thrown away my fair share of Broad Stack Test suites. Prior to deletion they'd become unmaintainable and constantly reported false negatives. ROI had become unquestionably negative. On the other hand I've found plenty of success using Broad Stack Tests I've written. For awhile I thought my success with Broad Stack Tests came from a combination of my dedication to making them as easy as possible to work with and that I never allowed more than a dozen of them.

I was wrong. I eventually figured out the trick to Broad Stack Tests: To be successful with Broad Stack Tests you have to be the person who wrote them. The complexity of Broad Stack Test infrastructure almost ensures that the original author will be the expert. Making changes to Broad Stack Test infrastructure is often as simple as moving a few variables. However, knowing which variables is a completely different problem. It's basically impossible to know what tiny changes to make unless you're the original author, or what I call the Broad Stack Test Whisperer (BSTW).

The fact that the Broad Stack Tests cannot be maintained

without the BSTW only solidifies my opinion that you should never have more than a dozen Broad Stack Tests. If the BSTW leaves, your best bet is to ditch the existing Broad Stack Tests and have the next BSTW write a version they're happy to own. Obviously you don't want this task to take a significant amount of time, thus limiting the number of Broad Stack Tests is in everyone's best interest.

Test Pyramid

> The test pyramid is a concept developed by Mike Cohn, described in his book Succeeding with Agile. Its essential point is that you should have many more low-level unit tests than high level end-to-end tests running through a GUI. –Martin Fowler, TestPyramid[23]

The Test Pyramid concept fits very well with the style I'm suggesting. In practice around 80%-90% of my tests are *Solitary Unit Tests*, 10%-20% are *Sociable Unit Tests*, and I have between one and twelve *Broad Stack Tests*.

---

[23]http://martinfowler.com/bliki/TestPyramid.html

Final Thoughts On ROI

When making implementation changes it's easy to see the value of unit tests. You can tweak the internals to your heart's content and the tests continue to provide feedback without requiring any coding attention. Conversely, making changes to the public API often results in spending as much or more time working with the test code. If you don't follow the patterns I've detailed in this book, I wouldn't be surprised to see you spending up to 80% of your time fixing tests during a public API change.

When the effort is split that drastically, it's natural to ask questions. Eventually, someone is going to ask: *Should we even bother writing Unit Tests?*

Many talented developers have proposed using exclusively Broad Stack Tests in the past. While this approach has its appeal, there are two hurdles that have thus far kept this proposal from gaining any traction. The main selling point is quite tempting: *You're able to make large architectural refactorings without changing any tests.* Unfortunately, the drawbacks are equally noteworthy: *Long Running Tests* (on the order of minutes and hours) and *Poor Defect Localization* (when things fail it can often take minutes or hours to find the root cause).

Despite these limitations, people continue to advance this approach. Still, I think it's safe to say unit tests will be around for the foreseeable future. I also believe that such a drastic approach is solving the problem in the wrong way. We shouldn't test everything with Unit or Broad Stack Tests. We should use all of the approaches, each where most appropriate, and most importantly:

The key is to test the areas that you are most worried about going wrong. That way you get the most benefit for your testing effort. –Martin Fowler, Refactoring

More...

review on good*reads*: http://review.wewut.com[24]

join the discussion group: http://group.wewut.com[25]

---

[24]http://review.wewut.com
[25]http://group.wewut.com